Joseph Ritson

A Select Collection of English Songs

In Three Volumes. Volume The Third

Joseph Ritson

A Select Collection of English Songs
In Three Volumes. Volume The Third

ISBN/EAN: 9783744767743

Printed in Europe, USA, Canada, Australia, Japan

Cover: Foto ©Thomas Meinert / pixelio.de

More available books at **www.hansebooks.com**

A SELECT COLLECTION OF ENGLISH SONGS.

IN THREE VOLUMES.
VOLUME THE THIRD.

—— APIS MATINÆ
MORE MODOQUE
GRATA CARPENTIS THYMA PER LABOREM
PLURIMUM.
HOR.

LONDON:
Printed for J. JOHNSON in St. Pauls Church-yard.
MDCCLXXXIII.

AIRS

TO THE

SONGS

IN

VOLUME I.

ADVERTISEMENT.

THE following Mufic was originally defigned to be bound up with the Volume to which it belongs. But it being thought that the appearance, convenience and utility of the Work would be more favoured by the prefent arrangement, the Reader is defired to excufe fuch little inaccuracys of reference as have been neceffarily produced by the alteration.

AIRS.

Class I.

Song I. Ah Chloris, could I now but fit.
Song II. When first upon your tender cheek.   Miſs Aikin.
No air to the firſt of theſe ſongs has been met with, and the other is not ſuppoſed to have been ſet, or to have any tune.

Song III.   When firſt I ſaw thee graceful move.
Set by ſignor Paſquali.

Song IV. I did but look and love a while. Otway.
Air unknown. *

Song V. Almerias face, her shape, her air. Visc. Molesworth.
Set by mr. John Alcock, organist of Plymouth.

Almerias face, her shape, her air, With charms resistless

wound the heart. In vain you for defence prepare; When from

her eyes love shoots his dart. So strong, so swift the arrow

flies, Such sure destruction flying makes, The bold op-poser

quickly dies, The fu—gitive it o—ver—takes.

Song VI. Ah gaze not on those eyes! forbear. Mrs. Cockburn.
Song VII. Oh forbear to bid me slight her. Hill.
No airs known.

Song VIII. While from my looks fair nymph you guess.
Set by mr. Dieupart.

While from my looks, fair nymph, you guess The secret

passions

---

* This and such like expressions (used for the sake of brevity) generally mean no more than that the tune has not come to the Editors knowledge. In some places they imply certainty. The different instances are not worth pointing out.

passions of my mind, My heavy eyes, you say confess A

heart to love and grief in—clin'd.

SONG IX. White as her hand fair Julia threw, Jenyns.
Was poorly set by a mr. Hawkins; and no other air is known.
SONG X. I smile at Love and all his arts. Vanbrugh.

I smile at Love and all his arts, The charming Cynthia

cry'd. Take heed, for Love has piercing darts, A

wounded swain re——ply———

———'d. Take heed, for Love has piercing darts, A

wound————ed swain reply—'d.

Song X. Whilst on those lovely looks I gaze. E. of Rochester.
Air unknown.

Song XI. I lik'd, but never lov'd, before.
Set by mr. William Turner.

I lik'd, but never lov'd, be—fore I saw thy charming face; Now ev'ry feature I adore, And dote on ev'ry grace. She ne'er shall know the kind desire, Which her cold look denies, Unless my heart that's all on fire Should sparkle thro' my eyes, Then if no gentle glance return A si—lent leave to speak, My heart which would for ever burn, Alas! must sigh and break.

Song XIII. My love was fickle once and changing. Addison.
Air not known.

Song XIV. I never saw a face till now:
Is set by capt. Pack, but the tune was not thought worth inserting.

Song XV. With women I have pass'd my days.
Air not known.

Song XVI.

SONG XVI. Why will Florella when I gaze.
   Was originally set by mr. Berenclow, whose composition has not been met with. There are notes to it in Bickhams Musical Entertainer, but they did not appear worth copying.

SONG XVII. Say Myra why is gentle love. Lord Lyttelton.
Set by mr. (since dr.) Howard.

Say My—ra why is gen—tle love, A stran—ger to that mind Which pi—ty and es—teem can move, Which can be just and kind? Is it because you fear to know The ills which love mo—lest? The ten—der care, the anx—ious fear, Which racks the am'rous breast? A—las! by some de—gree of woe, We ev'—ry bliss ob—tain. The

A 4

heart

heart can ne'er a transport know, Which ne——ver felt a pain.

SONG XVIII. In vain you tell your parting lover.   Prior.
Has been set by mr. Jackson, and others. The following is a minuet by Geminiani, to which it is very happily adapted.

Slow & tender.

In vain you tell your part——ing lov-er, You wish fair winds may waft him o——ver. Alas! what winds can hap——py prove, That bear me far from her I love. Alas! what dan——gers on the main Can equal those which I suf——tain, From slighted vows and cold disdain.

SONG XIX. Fain would you ease my troubled heart.
Air unknown.
SONG XX.

SONG XX. Why Delia ever when I gaze.

Larghetto.

Why De—lia ev—er when I gaze, Ap—pears in frowns that lovely face: Why are those smiles to me deny'd, That glad—den ev'—ry heart beside: In vain your eyes my flame reprove, I may de—spair, but still must love. In vain your eyes my flame re—prove, I may de—spair, but still must love.

SONG XXI. Ah blame me not if no despair. Wolseley.
SONG XXII. Wrong not sweet mistress of my heart. Raleigh.
SONG XXIII. You may cease to complain.
No airs known.
SONG XXIV. Saw you the nymph whom I adore. Carey.
Set by the author.
Larghetto.

Saw you the nymph whom I a——dore? Saw you

Song XXV. Tell me no more how fair she is. Bp. King.
No air known.

Song XXVI. The nymph that undoes me is fair and unkind.
Set by dr. Green.

Song XXVII.

Song XXVII. Take, oh take those lips away.
Set by mr. Galliard. (It has been likewise set by mr. Jackson of Exeter and others)

Slow

Take, oh! take those lips away, That so sweetly were forsworn; And those eyes the break of day, Lights that do mislead the morn. But my kisses bring again, Seals of love, though seal'd in vain. But my kiss—es bring again, Seals of love though seal'd in vain.

Song XXVIII. Go lovely rose. Waller.
Originally set by Henry Lawes, and since by others, but with little success.

Song XXIX. Go rose, my Chloes bosom grace. Gay.
Set by dr. Green.

Moderately slow.

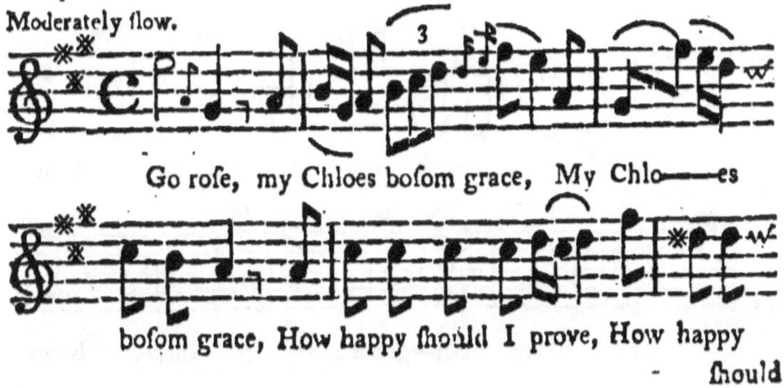

Go rose, my Chloes bosom grace, My Chlo——es bosom grace, How happy should I prove, How happy should

fra—gant ro—ses there. I see thy with'ring head reclin'd, With en—vy and de—spair, with en—vy and de—spair. One common fate we both must prove: You die with en—vy, I with love. One common fate we both must prove, You die with envy, I die with love. You die with envy, I with love. You with envy, I with love.

Song XXX. Mistaken fair, lay Sherlock by, E. of Chesterfield.

Andantino.

Mis-ta—ken fair, lay Sherlock by, His doctrine, doctrine.

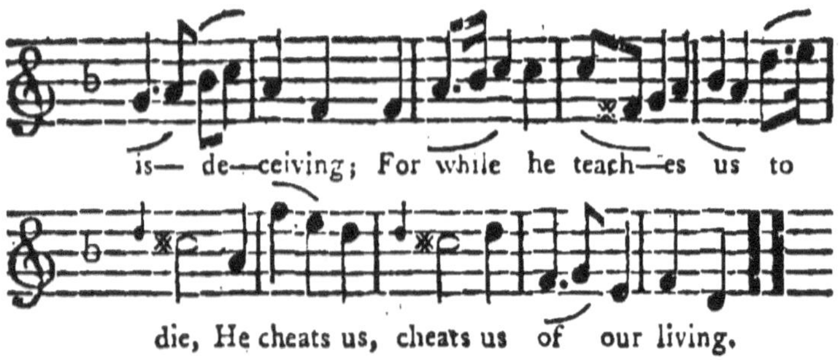

is—de—ceiving; For while he teach—es us to die, He cheats us, cheats us of our living.

Song XXXI. When first I fair Celinda knew.

When first I fair Ce—lin—da knew, Her kindness then was great; Her eyes I could with pleasure view, And friendly rays did meet. In all delights we past the time, That could di—version move; She oft would kind—ly hear me rhime Upon some others love, She oft would kind—ly hear me rhime Up—on some others love.

Song XXXII. When fair Serrena first I knew.
Song XXXIII. Fairest of thy sex and best.
No airs known.

Song. XXXIV.

Song XXXIV. Could you guess, for I ill can repeat. Wod-
(hull.

Song XXXV. If in that breast so good so pure. Moore.
Neither of these two pieces it is presumed ever had any air.

Song XXXVI. The silver rain, the pearly dew.
The editor has not been able to obtain a sight of the music to the entertainment from which this song is taken.

Song XXXVII. Whilst I am scorch'd with hot desire. Prior.

Song XXXVIII. 'Tis not your saying that you love. Mrs.
No airs known. (Behn.

Song XXXIX. Go tell Aminta, gentle swain. Dryden.
Set by mr. Robert King.

Go tell Aminta gentle swain, I would not die nor dare complain; Thy tuneful voice with numbers join, Thy voice will more prevail than mine; For souls op—press'd and dumb with grief, The Gods ordain'd this kind relief: That music should in sounds convey, What dying lovers dare not say.

Song XL.

SONG XL. Gentle love this hour befriend me.   Hill.
Set by count St. Germain.
Moderato.

Gentle Love this hour be—friend me, To my Eyes re-sign thy dart, Notes of melting mu-sic lend me, To dissolve a fro—zen heart. Chill as mountain snow her bo-som, Tho' I ten—der language use; 'Tis by cold in-diff—rence frozen, To my arms, and to my muse.

SONG XLI. I cannot change as others do.   E. of Rochester.
Airs not known.

SONG XLII. To melancholy thoughts a prey.   Mrs. Pilkington
See the music to the additional songs.

SONG XLIII. To all you ladies now at land.   E. of Dorset.

To all you ladies now at land, We men at sea
indite

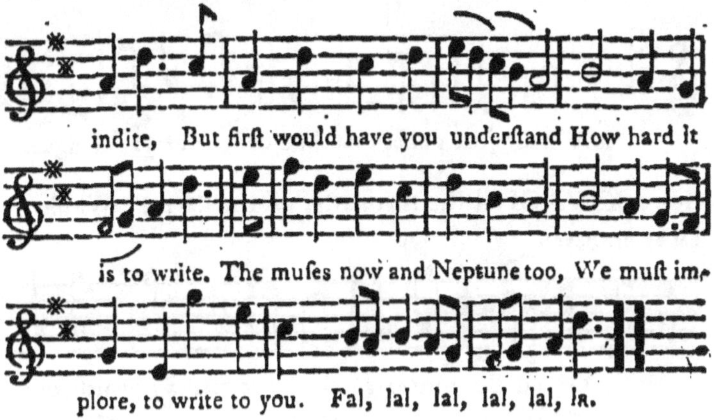

indite, But first would have you understand How hard it is to write. The muses now and Neptune too, We must implore, to write to you. Fal, lal, lal, lal, lal, la.

SONG XLIV. The heavy hours are almost past. L. Lyttelton.
Set by mr. Jackson of Exeter.
Moderately slow.

The heavy hours are almost past, That part my love and me; My longing eyes may hope at last Their on-ly wish to see. But how my Delia will you meet The man you've lost so long; Will love in all your pul——es beat And tremble on your tongue? Will

VOL. I.   B   love

love in all your pulses beat And tremble on your tongue.

Song XLV. Of all the torments, all the cares. Walsh.
Set by dr. Boyce.

Of all the torments, all the cares, By which our lives, are curst: Of all the plagues a lov——er bears Sure ri——vals are the worst. By part——ners in each o-ther kind, Af-flictions ea——si——er grow; In love alone we hate to find Com-pani——ons of our woe.

Song XLVI. Yes, fairest proof of beautys power. Prior.
No air known.

Song XLVII. Though cruel you seem to my pain. Carey.
Set by the author.

Though cruel you seem to my pain, And hate me be-
cause

cause I am true; Yet Phillis, you love a false swain, Who has o-ther nymphs in his view. En-joyment's a tri-fle to him, To me, what a heav'n would it be! To him but a woman you seem; But, ah! you're an an-gel to me.

SONG XLVIII. What fury does disturb my rest.
            No air known.

SONG XLIX. What state of life can be so blest. Dryden.
Was " sung by mrs. Hudson, and set by mr. John Eccles." *Durfey*. The notes have not been met with, but they are supposed to be like the rest of that gentlemans pantomimical performances, good for nothing.

SONG L. Say lovely dream, where could'st thou find. Waller.
The original music is unknown, and that of Anthony Neale is scarce worth preserving.

SONG LI. I'll range around the shady bow'rs. Carey.
Set by the author.

I'll range a-round the sha-dy bow-'rs, And ga-ther all the sweetest flow'rs: I'll strip the

garden

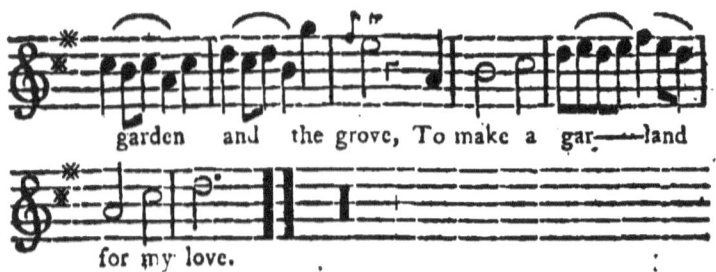

garden and the grove, To make a gar——land

for my love.

SONG LII. Why cruel creature why so bent. L. Lansdowne.
Set by mr. Flaston.

Why cruel crea-ture why so bent To vex a tender heart; To gold and ti-tle you re-lent, Love throws in vain his dar——t. Love throws in vain his dart.

SONG LIII. The sun was sunk beneath the hill.

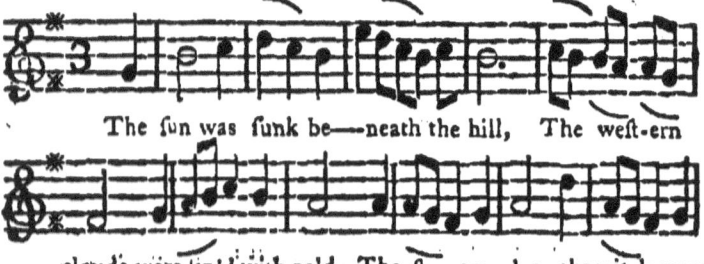

The sun was sunk be——neath the hill, The west-ern clouds were lin'd with gold; The sky was clear, the winds were still,

still, The flocks were pent within the fold; When from the si-lence of the grove, Poor Damon thus defpair'd of love.

Poor Damon thus defpair'd of love.

SONG LIV. I love, I dote, I rave with pain. *Otway.*
The Tune alluded to is not known. But the fong has been fet by dr. Boyce, though not in his happieft manner.

SONG LV. My time, o ye Mufes! was happily fpent. *Byron.*

My time, o ye mu—fes! was hap-pi-ly fpent, When
Ten thoufand foft pleafures I felt in my breaft, Sure

Phebe went with me where ev—er I went; But
never fond Shep-herd like Col-in was bleft:

now fhe is gone and has left me be—hind, What a

mar-vel-ous change on a fud-den I find; When
things

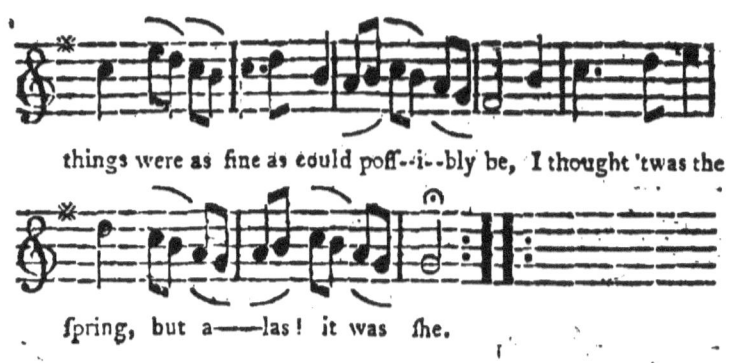

things were as fine as could poff--i--bly be, I thought 'twas the spring, but a——las! it was she.

Song LVI. To the brook and the willow that heard him complain. Rowe.

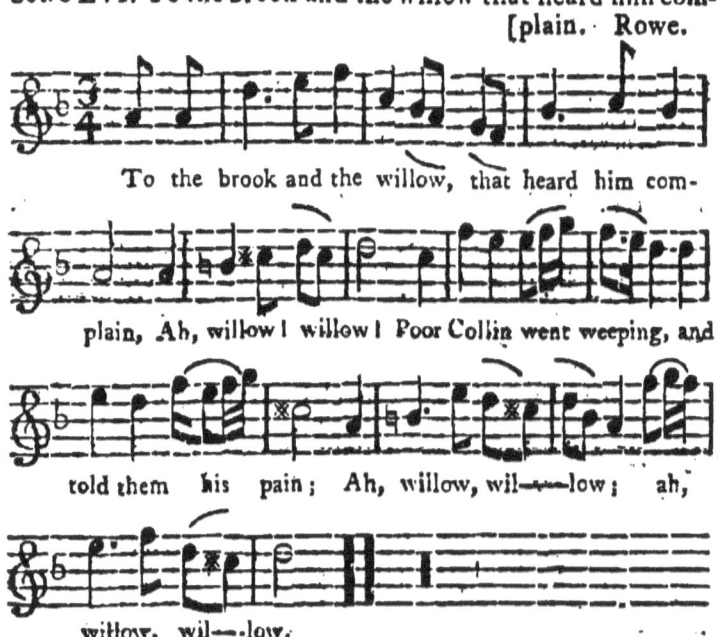

To the brook and the willow, that heard him complain, Ah, willow! willow! Poor Collin went weeping, and told them his pain; Ah, willow, wil——low; ah, willow, wil——low.

Song LVII. How gentle was my Damons air. Dalton.
Set by dr. Arne.

How gentle was my Damons air, Like funny
beams

beams his golden hair; His voice was like the nightingales:

More sweet his breath than flow'ry vales. How hard such

beauties to resign! And yet that cruel task is mine.

Amoroso.

On ev'ry hill, in ev'ry grove, Along the mar--gin

of each stream, Dear conscious scenes of former

love: I mourn and Damon is my theme. The

hills, the groves the streams re-main, But Da---mon

there I seek in vain. The hills, the groves, the

streams re—main, But Damon there I seek in vain.

From hill, from dale each charm is fled, Groves, flocks and

fountains please no more : Each flow'r in pi—ty

droops its head, All nature does my loss de-plore.

All, all re—proach the faithless swain, Yet Damon

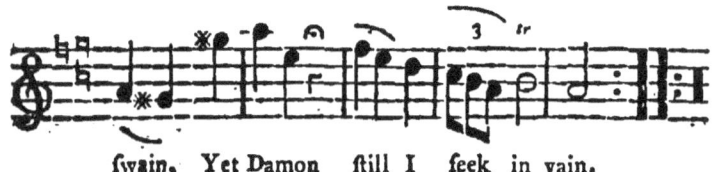

still I seek in vain. All, all reproach the faith-less

swain, Yet Damon still I seek in vain.

Song LVIII.

trees, And my hills are white over with sheep. I  seldom have met with a loss, Such health do my fountains be—stow; My fountains all border'd with  moss, Where the harebells and vio——lets grow,  ——Where the harebells and vi——o-lets grow.

Part III.
Tenderly.

Why will you my passion re—prove? Why  term it a fol——ly to grieve? Ere I

tell

nothing to do but to stray, I have nothing to do but to

weep. Yet do not my folly reprove, She was

fair, and my passion be——gun; She

smil'd and I could not but love; She was faithless and I am un-

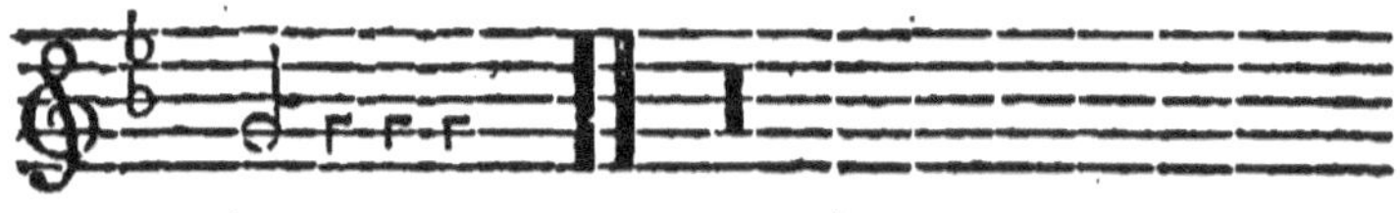

done.

SONG LIX. Despairing beside a clear stream.   Rowe.
Grim king of the ghosts make haste.

De-spairing beside a clear stream, A shepherd forsaken was

laid; And while a false nymph was his theme, A willow sup-

ported

ported his head; The wind that blew over the plain, To his  sighs with a sigh did re-ply: And the brook in return to his pain, Ran mournfully murmuring by.

Song LX. Come all ye youths whose hearts e'er bled. Otway.

The following are supposed to be the original notes. There is a later, but not much superior air by dr. Boyce.

Come all ye youths whose hearts e'er bled, By cruel  Beautys pride; Bring each a garland on his head,  Let none his sorrows hide: But hand in hand a-round me move, Singing the sad-est tales of love, And  see when your complaints you join, If all your wrongs

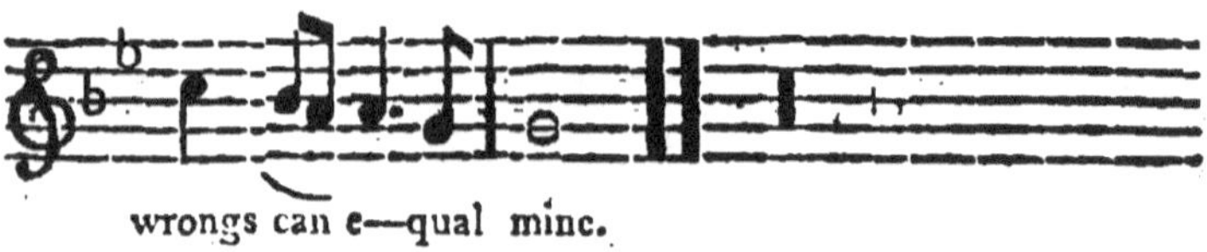

wrongs can e—qual mine.

SONG LXI. Grim king of the ghosts make haste.
See air LIX.

SONG LXII. One night when all the village slept. Scroope.
Set by mr. Oswald.

One night when all the vil—lage slept, Myr—tillos sad de—spair, The wretched shep—herd waking kept: To tell the woods his care. Be—gone, (said he) fond thoughts be-gone, Eyes give your sor—rows o'er, Why should you waste your love for one Who thinks on you no more.

SONG LXIII.

Song LXIII. Ah! Damon, dear shepherd, adieu.

Ah! Damon, dear shep-herd a—dieu! By love and first na—ture al-ly'd! To-gether in fondness we grew, Ah! would we to—gether had dy'd, Ah! would we to-gether had dy'd! For thy faith, which re-sembled my own, For thy love which was spot-less and true, For the joys we to-ge——ther have known, Ah! Damon, dear shep-herd a——dieu, Ah! Damon, dear shepherd, a-dieu.

Song LXIV.

SONG LXV. 'Twas when the seas were roaring.   Gay.

Set by mr. Handel.

'Twas when the seas were roaring, With hollow blasts of

wind,   A damsel lay deploring,   All   on   a   rock re-

clin'd: Wide o'er the foaming billows,   She cast a wistful

look;   Her head was crown'd with   wil——lows,   That

trembled o'er the   brook.

THE SAME SONG, Set by mr. Jackson of Exeter, under the title of *Susanna.* The extreeme sweetness of the air of this cantata, and the masterly stile of the whole composition, must be the editors apology for inserting it contrary to his professed design, and immediately after so capital a piece as mr. Handels original music.

Recitative.

Largo andante.   'Twas when the seas were roaring, With hollow blasts of

VOL. I.   C   wind,

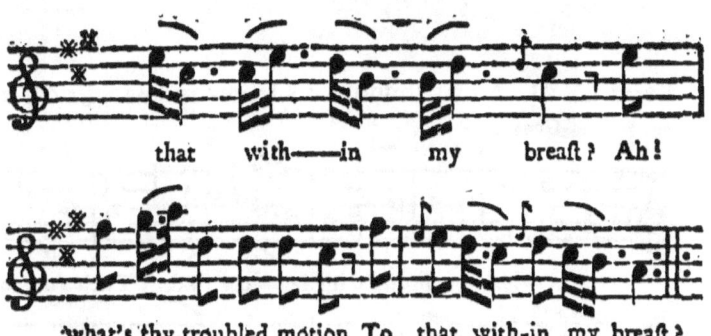
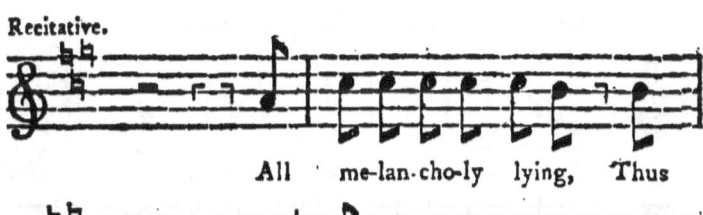

SONG LXVI. Alexis shunn'd his fellow swains. Prior.
Set by mr. Gouge.

A—lex—is shunn'd his fel—low swains, Their ru—ral sports and jocund strains. (Heav'n guard us all from Cu—pids bow!) He lost his crook, he left his flocks, And wand'ring thro' the lone—ly rocks, He nou—rish'd end—less woe.

SONG LXVII. Hard by the hall, our masters house.
No air known.

SONG LXVIII. Of Leinster fam'd for maidens fair. Tickell.

May be sung, with great propriety, to the fine old tune of The Children in the Wood. See the music in Class III. Song XLI. There is another air for it in the Musical Miscellany, Vol. 1. p. 4. And one or two more it is believed may be found elsewhere. But as none of these compositions is either distinguishable for its merit or appears to be peculiarly connected with the words, the editor took the liberty to omit them.

SONG LXIX. Come listen to my tender tale. Shenstone.
No air known.

CLASS II.

Class II.

Song I. Fairest isle, all isles excelling. Dryden.

Set by mr. Henry Purcell.

Song II. Come thou rosy dimpled boy. Parrat.

Come thou ro-sy dimpled boy, Source of ev'ry heart-felt joy, Leave the blissful bow'rs a-while, Paphos and the Cyprian isle; Visit Britains

rocky

Come thou ro-sy dimpled boy.

Come thou ro-sy dimpled boy.

Come thou ro-sy dimpled boy.

SONG III. Ask me not how calmly I.

Ask me not how calm—ly I All the cares of life de—fy? How I baffle hu-man woes? Woman, wo-man, wo—man knows. You may live and laugh as I, You like me may care de—fy; All the pangs the heart en—dures,

Woman,

Woman, woman, wo—man cures.

SONG IV. Ah! how sweet it is to love. Dryden.

Set by mr. Henry Purcell.

Ah! how sweet, Ah! how sweet, how sweet it is to love; Ah! Ah! Ah! how gay is young desire. And what pleas—ing pains, and what pleas—ing pains we prove, When first, when first we feel a lov—ers fire. Pains of love are sweet——er far, Than all, all, all,

Song V. Love's no irregular desire.
Air unknown.

Song VI. Love's a gentle gen'rous passion. Carey.
Set by the author.

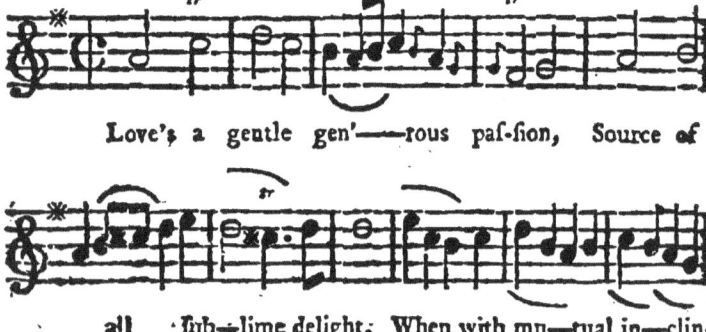

ation, Two fond hearts in one u—nite, Two fond

hearts in one u—nite.

SONG VII. O how vain is every bleſſing.
           The muſic of this ſong has not been met with.

SONG VIII. Honeſt lover whatſoever. Suckling.

SONG IX. Tell me Damon, doſt thou languiſh?
           No airs known.

SONG X. Come here fond youth, whoe'er thou be. Miſs Aikin
           Is ſuppoſed never to have been ſet, nor to have any tune.

SONG XI. A maxim this, amongſt the wiſe.
           No air known.

SONG XII. Over the mountains and over the waves:

Over the mountains and over the waves, Un-der the

fountains and under the graves, Under floods that are

                                          deepeſt

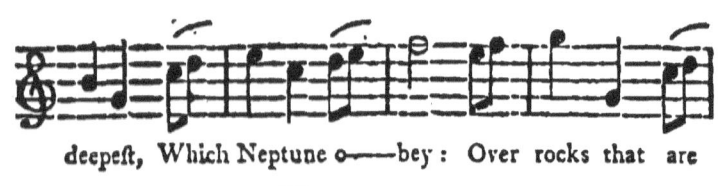

deepest, Which Neptune o——bey: Over rocks that are

steepest, Love will find out the way.

Song XIII. Oft on the troubled oceans face.   Theobald.
Set by mr. Galliard.

Oft on the trou——bled o——ceans face, Loud

stormy winds a——rise; The mur-m'ring sur——ges

swell apace, And clouds ob——scure the skies.

But, when the tempests rage is o'er, Soft breezes smooth the

main; The billows cease to lash the shore, And

all

all is calm again. Not so in fond and am'rous souls. If ty-rant Love once reigns, There one e—ter—nal tempest rolls, And yields unceasing pains. Ah, cruel god! our peace re—store, Or wound us with thy shafts no more: Ah, cruel god! ah, cruel god! our peace re-store, Or wound us with thy shafts no more.

SONG XIV. The flame of love assuages.   Carey.
Air unknown.

SONG XV. Love's a dream of mighty treasure.
Set by dr. Arne.

Love's a dream of might—y treasure, Which in fancy

Song XVI. Freedom is a real treasure. Wolsely.

Moderato.

Freedom is a real treasure, Love a dream, all false and vain; Love a dream, all false and vain; Short, uncer—tain is the pleasure, Sure and lasting is the pain, Sure - - - and last——ing is the pain.

Song XVII. Ye happy swains whose hearts are free. Etherege
Set by mr. Damasene.

Ye hap-py swains whose hearts are free, From loves im—pe—rial chain: Hence forth be warn'd and taught

taught by me, And taught by me, T' a-

void th'inchanting pain. Fa-tal the wolves to

trembling flocks, Sharp winds to blossoms prove; To

careless seamen hidden roks, To human qui—et

love.

SONG XVIII. *From sweet bewitching tricks of love.*
Set by dr. Arne.
Brisk.

From sweet be—witching tricks of love, Young

men your hearts se——cure; Lest from the paths of

sense

sense you rove, In dotage pre—ma—ture. In dotage pre—ma—ture. Look at each lass through wisdoms glass, Nor trust the na—ked eye; Gallants beware, look sharp, take care! The blind eat many a fly, The blind eat many a fly.

Song XIX. Old Chaucer once to this re-echoing grove.
[Smart.

Set by dr. Arne.
Recitative.

Old Chaucer once to this re-echoing grove, Sung of "The sweet

ble and mad: Save women, they, we must confess, Are

miracles of stedfastness; And ev'ry witty, pretty,

witty, pretty, dame Bears for her motto, for her motto,

Bears for her motto STILL THE SAME.

The flow'rs that in the vale are seen, The white, the yellow,

blue and green. In brief complexion id—ly gay Still

set with ev'ry sett-ing day; Dispers'd by wind, or

chill'd

chill'd by frost, Their odour's gone, their colour lost: But

what is true, though passing strange, The women never

fade or change.

V. 3. To the common time movement.
V. 4. To the jig movement.

An hundred mouths, an hundred tongues, An

hundred pair of i-ron longs; Five heralds, and

five thousand cryers, With throats whose ac-cent

never tires, never tires, never tires; Ten speaking-trumpets,

of

CLASS III.

SONG I. He that loves a rosy cheek. Carew.

Was set by Henry Lawes, whose compositions, however admirable they might be in his own age, will command very little respect in the present.

SONG II. Vain are the charms of white and red. Pulteney.

SONG III. Though, Flavia, to my warm desire.

SONG IV. Belinda, see from yonder flow'rs.

No airs known.

SONG V. It is not that I love you less. Waller.

Appears to have been originally set by Henry Lawes. There are likewise notes to it by mr. Oswald; but the following tune is the composition of count St. Germain.

It is not that I love you less, Than when be-

fore your feet I lay: But, to pre——vent the

sad in————crease Of hope——less love, I

keep a——way. In vain, a—— ——las! for

every

every thing, Which I have known be—long to you, Your form does to my fancy bring, And makes my old wounds bleed anew, And makes my old wounds bleed a—new.

SONG VI. Yes, Daphne, in your face I find.
No air known.

SONG VII. In Chloris all soft charms agree. How.
Set by mr. Henry Purcell; but the music was not judged worth inserting.

SONG VIII. You say, at your feet I have wept in despair. [Mendez.
Set by dr. Boyce.

You say, at your feet I have wept in de-spair, And

vow'd that no angel was ev- - er so fair: How could you be- lieve

lieve all the nonsense I spoke? What know we of angels?—

I meant it in joke, I meant it in joke. What

know we of angels?— I meant it in joke.

SONG IX. Know Celia, (since thou art so proud.) Carew.
No air known.

SONG X. Why d'ye with such disdain refuse. Vanbrook.
Set by mr. Leveridge.

Why d'ye with such dis-dain refuse, An humble lovers

plea? Since heav'n denies you pow'r to chuse, You

ought to value me. Ungrateful mistress of a heart Which

I so free—ly gave, Though weak your bow, though blunt your dart, I soon resign'd your slave.

SONG XI. Once more Loves mighty charms are broke. Sedley.
Not known.

SONG XII. Come, let us now resolve at last. D. of Buckingham.
No airs known.

SONG XIII. False though she be to me and love. Congreve.
Was set by a mr. Gunn, but his music is not worth preserving, and no other air has been met with.

SONG XIV. If 'tis joy to wound a lover. Addison.
Set by dr. Arnold.

If 'tis joy to wound a lover, How much more to give him ease, When his passion you discover, Ah! how pleasing 'tis to please. If 'tis

joy

Song XV. Away with these self-loving lads. Lord Brooke.
Set by mr. Dowland, the lutanist. (about 1600).

XVI. Chloris

SONG XVI. Cloris, 'twill be for eithers reft. Bulteel.
No air known.

SONG XVII. Fair Iris I love, and hourly I die. Dryden.

Song XVIII. I love thee, by heavens, I cannot say more.
[Concanen.

I love thee, by heavens, I can-not say more; Then

set not my passion a cool-ing; If thou

yield'st not at once I must e'en give thee o'er, For

I'm but a nov—ice at fool—ing.

Song XIX. I'm not one of your fops, who to please a coy
[lass. Budgell.
Air unknown.

Song XX. Let not Love on me bestow. Steel.

Was set, in a most laboured mechanical manner, by Daniel Purcell, for mrs. Harris; but his music was not thought worthy of insertion. It is preserved in the 6th volume of Durfeys Pills to purge melancholy.

Song XXI. Give me more love, or more disdain. Carew.

Was originally set by Henry Lawes. (See his *Ayres and Dialogues*, book 2d. fol. 1669.

Song XXII. If love be life, I long to die. Davison.
No air known.

Song XXIII.

SONG XXIII. Shall I, wasting in despair. Wither.

The original music is not known; and of the later airs none appeared worth copying.

SONG XXIV. Shall I, like an hermit, dwell. Raleigh.

Not known.

SONG XXV. Why so pale and wan, fond lover? Suckling.

Sung by mrs. Cross in the Mock Astrologer: Set by mr. Ramondon. It was likewise set by dr. Arne, but the work of neither composer appeared to be worthy of insertion.

SONG XXVI. Ye little Loves, that round her wait.

Ye lit—tle loves that round her wait, To bring me tid—ings of my fate, As Ce—lia on her pil—low lies, Ah! gent-ly whisper Stre--phon dies. If this will

not

SONG XXVII. 'Tis now since I sat down before. Suckling.
Air unknown.

SONG XXVIII. The merchant to secure his treasure. Prior.
Was poorly set by dr. Green. The following music is by mr. Jackson, of Exeter.

to the Loves a-round, Remark'd how ill we all dis——fem——bled.

Song XXIX. In vain, dear Chloe, you fuggeft. Yonge.

Set by mr. Dieupart.

In vain, dear Chlo——e, you fuggeft, That I in-con-ftant have pofs-efs'd, Or lov'd a fair——er fhe; Would you, with eafe, at once be cur'd Of all the ills you've long en——dur'd, Con-fult your glafs and me.

Song XXX,

Song XXX. Should some perverse malignant star.
No air known.

Song XXXI. Dear Chloe, how blubber'd is that pretty face!
[Prior.
This has been set, but no air of merit has occurred.

Song XXXII. When gentle Celia first I knew. Miss Aikin.
Never set.

Song XXXIII. I grant, a thousand oaths I swore. Bulteel.

Song XXXIV. Margarita first possess'd. Cowley.

Song XXXV. Why we love, and why we hate. Philips.
No airs known.

Song XXXVI. Tom loves Mary passing well.

Tom loves Mary passing well, And Mary she loves

Har—ry, But Harry sighs for bon—ny Bell, And

finds his love mis—-car—ry; For bon—ny Bell for

Thomas

Song XXXVII. Well met, pretty nymph, says a jolly young
[swain.

venture

venture to ask you fair maid—en, which way? Then  straight to this question the nymph did re-ply, With a  smile on her look and a leer in her eye, I am  come from the village, and homeward I go; And  now gentle shepherd, pray why would you know?

Song XXXVIII. A courting I went to my love.

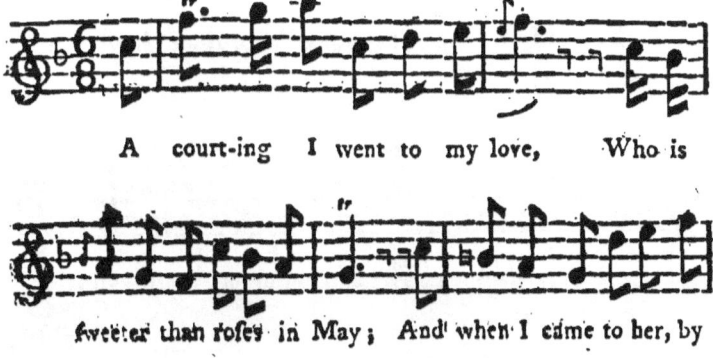

A court-ing I went to my love, Who is sweeter than roses in May; And when I came to her, by Jove,

Jove,· The de-vil a word could I say. I

walk'd with her in-to the gar—den, There fully intending to

woo her; But may I be ne'er worth a farthing, If of

love I said a--ny thing to her.

Song XXXIX. Distracted with care. Walsh.
Air unknown.

Song XL. My name is honest Harry.
The tune is *Robin Rowser*, which has not been met with.

Song XLI. My passion is as mustard strong. Gay?
Tune, *Babes in the wood.*

My pas-sion is as mustard strong, I sit all sober

sad,

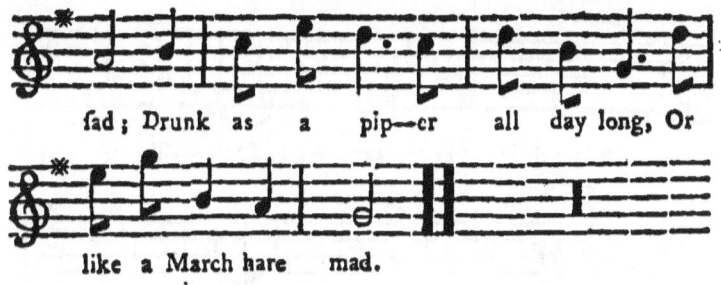

Song XLII. A cobler there was, and he liv'd in a stall.
See the tune in Part III. Song. LXI.

Class IV.

Song I. As Amoret with Phillis sat. Sedley.

E 4

Song II. When Phillis watch'd her harmless sheep. Etherege.
Air unknown.

Song III. From place to place forlorn I go. Steel.

Song IV.

what is too ten-der to name.

SONG V. If love and reason ne'er agree.
Not known.

SONG VI. Ah! why must words my flame reveal?
Set by mr. Jackson of Exeter.

Ah why must words my flame reveal, Why

needs my Damon bid me tell, What all my actions

prove? A blush whene'er I meet his eye, When-

e'er I hear his name, a sigh Betrays my secret

love. When-e'er I hear his name, a sigh Be-

trays my secret love.

SONG VII.

SONG VII. If Cupid once the mind poſſeſs.
Air not met with.

SONG VIII. How hardly I conceal'd my tears. Mrs. Wharton.
No air known.

SONG IX. Boaſt not miſtaken ſwain thy art.

SONG X. Too plain, dear youth, thoſe tell-tale eyes. Jenyns.
Set by mr. Howard.

SONG XIII. On the brow of a hill a young shepherdess dwelt.
[Miss M. Jones.

Was originally set by mr. Lampe. But the following is the more favourite music, composed by mr. Howard.

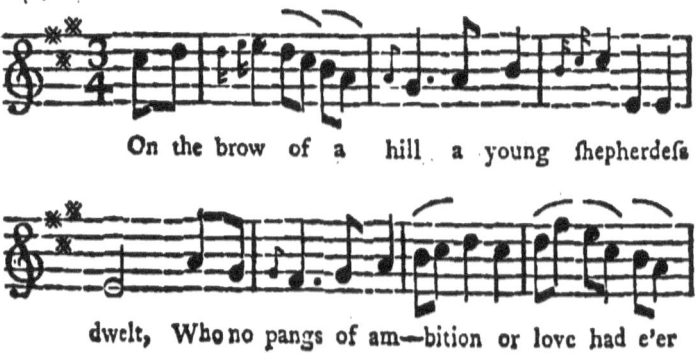

felt

Song XIV. When lovely woman stoops to folly. Goldsmith.
No air.

CLASS V.

CLASS V.

Song I. Sweet are the charms of her I love. Booth.

Set by mr. Leveridge.

Song II. My days have been so wond'rous free. Parnell.

This song has been set by mr. Jackson of Exeter, whose music will be found among the airs to the additional pieces, *(Ab cruel maid how hast thou chang'd)* The following seem to be the original notes.

little

little birds that fly With careless ease from tree to tree, Were but as bless'd as I. Ask gliding waters, if a tear Of mine increas'd their stream, Or ask the flying gales, if e'er I lent, I lent a sigh to them.

SONG III. Stella, darling of the muses. Mrs. Pilkington.
"To a celebrated air in Demetrius."

Stella, darling of the Muses, Fairer than the blooming spring; Sweetest theme the poet chouses,

VOL. I.   F   When

When of thee he strives to sing, When of thee he strives to sing. While my soul with wonder trac—es All thy charms of face and mind, All the beauties, all the graces of thy sex in thee I find, Of thy sex in thee I find.

SONG IV. When Delia on the plain appears. L. Lyttelton.
Set by Mr. Holcombe.

When Delia on the plain appears, Aw'd by a thousand tender fears, I would approach

proach but dare not move: Tell me, my heart, if this be love? Tell me, tell me, my heart, if this be love?

Song V. As he lay in the plain, his arm under his head.

Song VI. Dejected as true converts die. D. of Buckingham.

Song VII. Sighing and languishing I lay. Ditto.

Song VIII. Phillis, men say that all my vows. Sedley.
No airs known.

Song IX. I told my nymph, I told her true. Shenstone.
Set by mr. Joseph Harris, organist of Ludlow.

I told my nymph, I told her true, My

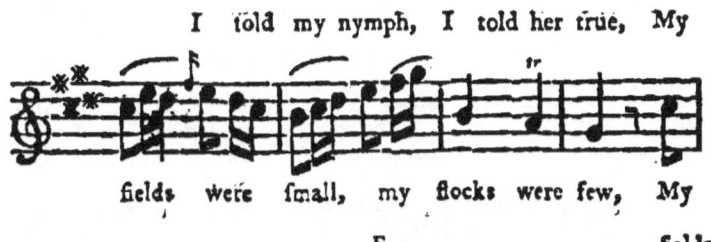

fields were small, my flocks were few, My fields

fields were small, my flocks were few; While

fault'ring accents spoke my fear, That Flavia

might not prove sin—cere, While fault'ring

accents spoke my fear, That Flavia might not

prove sin——cere.

SONG X. O had I been by fate decreed. Baker.

Set by mr. Abiel Whichello. (It may be also sung to dr. Howards tune in Love in a Village.)

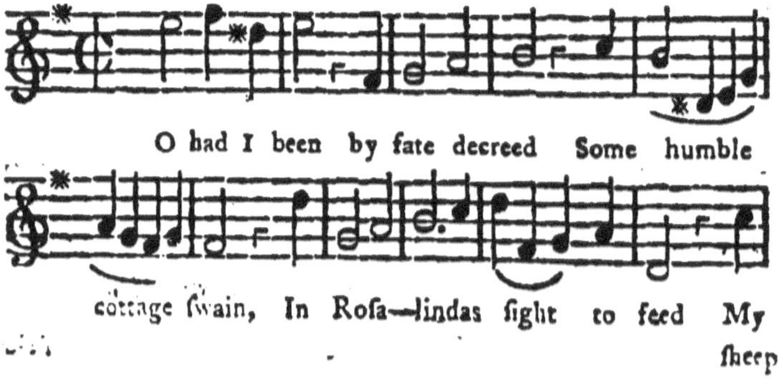

O had I been by fate decreed Some humble

cottage swain, In Rosa—lindas sight to feed My sheep

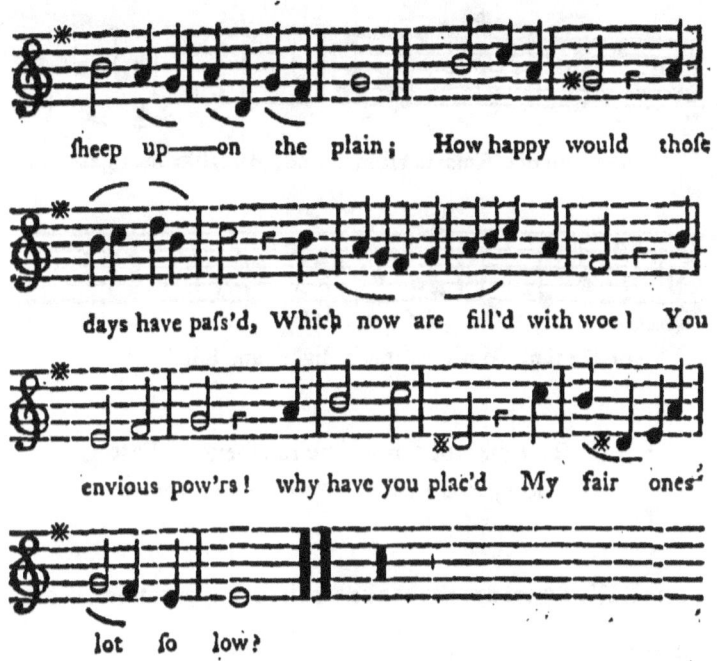

Song XI. We all to conquering beauty bow.

Set by dr. John Blow.

F 3   met

met with one Amazes all mankind; And, like men gaz—ing

on the fun, With too much light am blind.

Song XII. Tell me not I my time misspend. Eaton.
Was set by Henry Lawes. No other air is known.

Song XIII. Sweet are the banks when spring perfumes. Woty.

Allegretto

Piano.

Sweet are the banks when spring perfumes The

verdant plants and laughing flow'rs; Fragrant the vi—o—let

as it blooms, And sweet the bloss—oms after show'rs,

Fragrant

kisses are of her I love, The kisses are of her I love, The kisses are of her I love.

SONG XIV. For me my fair a wreath has wove. *Garrick.*
Set by mr. Giardini.

Siciliana.

For me my fair a wreath has wove, Where rival flow'rs in

union meet, Where rival flow'rs in union meet; As

oft she kiss'd this gift of love, Her breath gave sweetness

to

to the sweet, As oft she kiss'd this gift of love, Her

breath gave sweetness to the sweet, Her breath gave sweetness

to the sweet,

SONG XV. Cease to blame my melancholy. Moore.

No air.

SONG XVI. That which her slender waist confin'd. Waller.
Air unknown.

SONG XVII. Let the ambitious ever find. E. of Dorset.
The only notes to this song which have been discovered possess too little merit to intitle them to a place in this collection.

SONG XVIII. Bless'd as th' immortal gods is he. Philips.
Was set by a mr. Stubley, and (doubtless in a masterly stile) by mr. Jackson of Exeter. It is however more usually sung to the following very beautiful Scotch

Tune: *I wish my love were in a mire.*

Slow.

Bless'd as th' immortal gods is he, The youth

youth who fondly sits by thee, And hears and sees thee, all the while, Softly speak, and sweetly smile. 'Twas this depriv'd my soul of rest, And rais'd such tumults in my breast; For while I gaz'd, in transport tofs'd, My breath was gone, my voice was lost.

Song XIX. My goddess Lydia, heav'nly fair. E. of Rochester.

My god——ess Lydia, heav'n—ly fair, As lilies sweet, as soft as air; Let

loose

loose thy tresses, - spread thy charms, And to my love give fresh alarms.

SONG XX. On Belvidera's bosom lying.
Air unknown.

SONG XXI. To be gazing on those charms. Carey.
Set by the author.

To be gaz——ing on those charms,

To be fold——ed in those arms,

To u——nite my lips with those

Whence e—tern——al sweetness flows; To be

lov'd

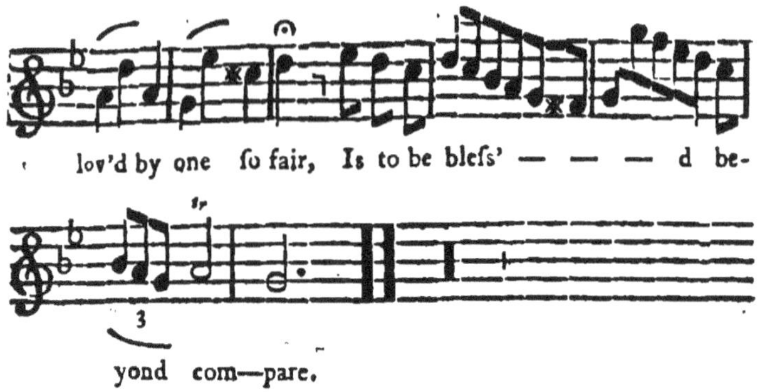
lov'd by one ſo fair, Is to be bleſs' — — — d be-
tr
3
yond com—pare.

SONG XXII. The bird that hears her neſtlings cry.

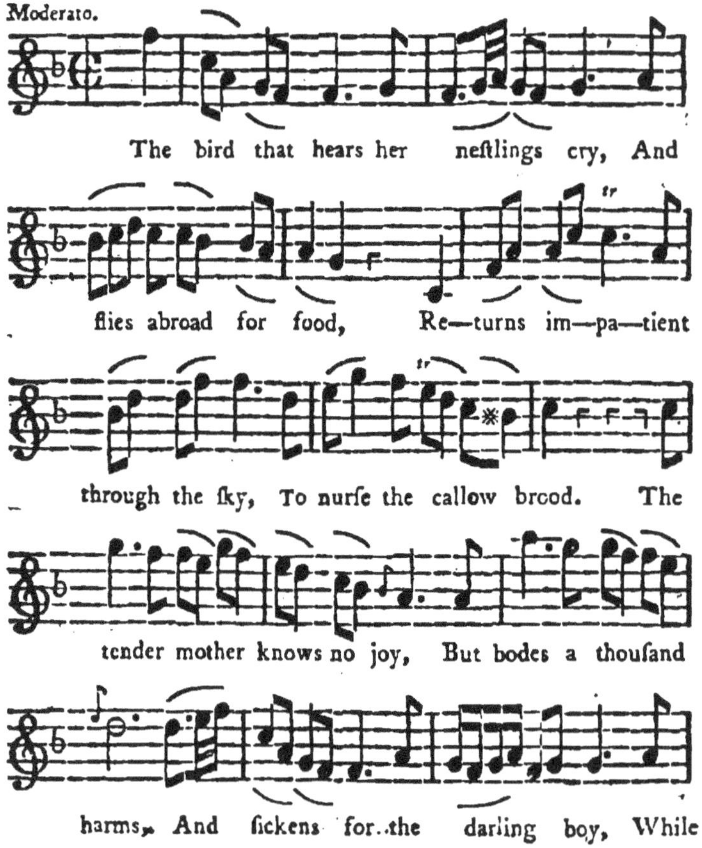
Moderato.
The bird that hears her neſtlings cry, And
flies abroad for food, Re—turns im—pa—tient
through the ſky, To nurſe the callow brood. The
tender mother knows no joy, But bodes a thouſand
harms, And ſickens for the darling boy, While

absent

ab— — —sent from her arms.

Song XXIII. From all uneasy passions free. D. of Buckingham.
No air known.

Song XXIV. Once more I'll tune the vocal shell. Garrick.

Once more I'll tune the vo——cal shell, To  hills and dales my pas——sion tell; A  flame which time can nev - - - er quell, That  burns for love——ly Peg——gy. Yet greater bards the  lyre should hit; For, say what subject is more fit, Than

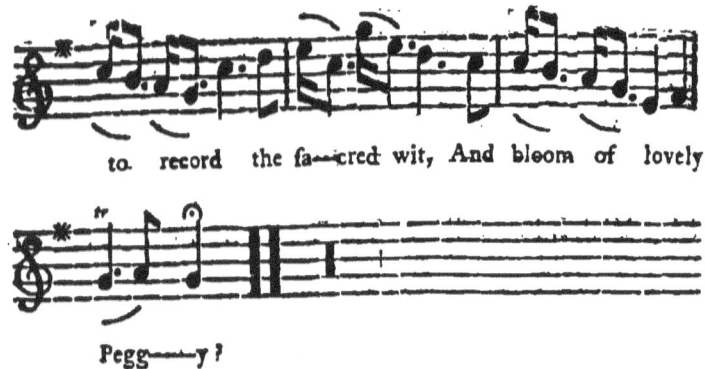

to record the sa—cred wit, And bloom of lovely Pegg——y?

SONG XXV. The silver moons enamour'd beam. Cunningham.
Set by mr. Battishill.

The silver moons en—amour'd beam Steals

soft——ly through the night, To wanton with the wind——ing stream, And kiss re——flect——ed light To beds of down go

balm—y sleep, ('Tis where you've seldom been) May's vi—gil while the shep—herds keep, With Kate of Ab—er—deen, With Kate of Ab—er—deen, With Kate of Ab—er—deen.

Song XXVI. The western sky was purpled o'er. Shenstone.
Set by mr. Dibdin.

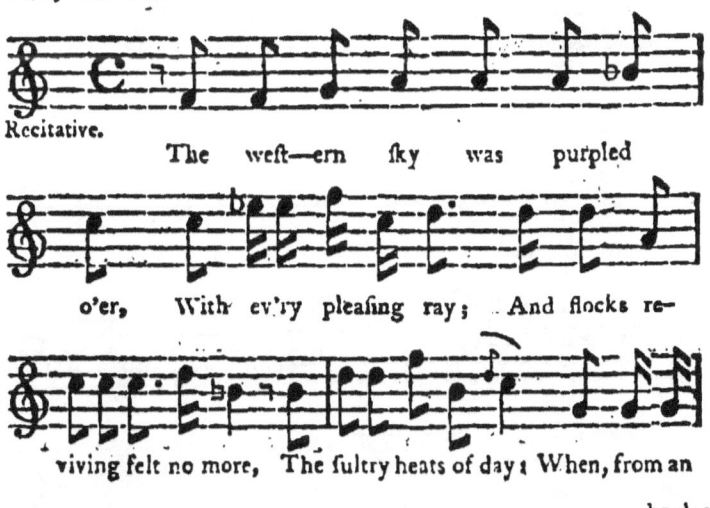

Recitative. The west—ern sky was purpled o'er, With ev'ry pleasing ray; And flocks reviving felt no more, The sultry heats of day; When, from an

hazles

faw

saw fair Eshams dale   And ev'ry blessing find its way,   To Nan——cy of the Vale.

Song XXVII. Not, Celia, that I juster am. Sedley.

Song XXVIII. Not the soft sighs of vernal gales. Johnson.
No airs known.

Song XXIX. The gentle swan with graceful pride. Cunningham.
Set by dr. Arne.

Andante. The gentle swan, with graceful pride, Her glossy plumage laves, And sailing down the sil——ver tide, Divides the whisp'ring waves,

waves — — — Divides the whisp'ring waves. The silver tide - -, that wand'ring flows, Sweet, sweet to the bird must be! But not so sweet, blithe Cupid knows, As Delia is to me, As De - - - lia is to me.

Song XXX. If wine and music have the pow'r. Prior.
Air unknown.

Song XXXI. Come, Chloe, and give me sweet kisses. Hanbury [Williams?

Brisk.
Come, Chloe, and give me sweet kisses, For
sweeter

Song XXXII. When charming Teraminta sings.
Air unknown.

Song XXXIII. Thus Kitty beautiful and young. Prior?

Set by dr. Arne.

Andante Allegro.

Thus Kitty, beautiful and young, and wild as colt un-

tam'd; Bespoke the fair from whom she sprung, With

little rage inflam'd: In—flam'd with rage at

sad restraint, Which wise mama ordain'd, And

sorely vex'd to play the saint, Whilst wit and beauty

reign'd, Whilst wit and beauty reign — —

—'d

—'d   And sorely vex'd to play the saint,   Whilst wit and beauty reign'd.

Song XXXVI. Stella and Flavia, ev'ry hour. Mrs. Pilkington.

Stella and Flavia, ev'—ry hour, Do various hearts sur——prise; In Stellas foul lies all her pow'r; And Flavias in her eyes. In Stellas foul lies all her pow'r; And Flavias in her eyes.

eyes. More bound—less Flavias conquests are, And Stellas more con—fin'd; All can dis—cern a

face that's fair, But few a lovely mind.

Song XXXV. The shape alone let others prize. Akenside.
No air known.

Song XXXVI. When innocence and beauty meet.

When innocence and beauty meet, To add to lovely

female grace. Ah, how beyond ex—pression sweet Is
ev'ry

ev'—ry fea—ture of the face. By

virtue, ripen'd from the bud, The flow'r an-ge—lic

odours breeds, The fragrant charms of being good, Makes

gawdy vice to smell like weeds.

Song XXXVII. My dear mistress has a heart. E. of Rochester.
Set by dr. Arne.

My dear mistress has a heart, Soft as

those kind looks she gave me, When with love's re-

listless

Song XXXVIII.

Song XXXIX. Yes I'm in love, I feel it now. Whitehead.

Set by dr. Arne.

Gently. Yes I'm in love, I feel it now, And Ce—lia has un—done me, And Ce—lia has un—done me; And yet I'll swear, I can't tell how, The pleasing plague stole on me: And yet I'll swear I can't tell how The pleasing plague stole on me, The pleasing plague stole on me.

Song XL.

Song XL. Of all the girls that are so smart. Carey.
Set by the author.

Of all the girls that are so smart, There's none like

pretty Sally; She is the darling of my

heart, And she lives in our alley.

There's ne'er a la——dy in the

land, Is half so sweet as Sally;

She is the darling of my heart, And she lives in

our alley.

Song XLI. All in the downs the fleet was moor'd. Gay.

Set by mr. Leveridge.

All in the Downs the fleet was moor'd, The

streamers waving in the wind, When black-ey'd Susan

came onboard. Oh! where shall I my true love find?

Tell me, ye jovial sailors, tell me true, If my sweet

William, If my sweet William sails a—mong the

crew!

Song XLII.

SONG XLII. Thou rising sun, whose gladsome ray. Steel.

Set by dr. Arne.

SONG XLIII. Waft me some soft and cooling breeze. [Croxal.

Set by Harry Carey.

wide

wide spreading trees, Re—pell the dog-stars rag—ing heat. Where tufted grafs and mofsy beds Af—ford a rural calm re—pofe. Where woodbines hang their dewy heads, And fragrant sweets a—round dis—close.

Song XLIV. O Nancy, wilt thou go with me. Percy.

Set by mr. Carter.

Largo andante expreffivo.

O Nan—cy wilt thou go with me, Nor figh to leave the flaunting town, Can fi——lent glens have charms

thou wert fairest, Where thou wert fair——est of the fair.

Song XLV. Come, dear Pastora, come away. Miss Whateley.
No air known.

Song XLVI. Hail to the myrtle shade. Lee.

Hail to the myrtle shade, All hail to the nymps of the fields, Kings would not here invade the pleasures that vir—tue yields: Beauty here opens her arms To soften the languishing mind, And Phillis unlocks all her charms: Ah, Phillis, ah why so kind?

Song XLVII.

Song XLVII. Come, dear Amanda, quit the town.

Come, dear A—man—da, quit the town, And to the ru—ral hamlets fly; Behold, the wint'ry storms are gone, A gentle radiance glads the sky. The birds a——wake, the flow'rs appear, Earth spreads a ver—dant couch for thee; 'Tis joy and music all we hear, 'Tis love and beauty all we see.

Song XLVIII. Haste, my rein-deer, and let us nimbly go. [Steel?

No air known.

Song XLIX. When here, Lucinda, first we came. E. of
[Middlesex.

Set by mr. Holcombe.

When here, Lu—cinda, first we came, Where Arno rolls his sil — — ver stream, How blithe the nymphs, the swains how gay, Content in—spir'd each rural lay. The birds in livelier concert sung, The grapes in thick — — er clusters hung; All look'd as joy could ne—ver fail, Among the sweets of Arnos vale.

Song L.

Song L. **Be still, o ye winds, and attentive ye swains.** Moore

Set by dr. Arne.

Gently. Be still, o ye winds, and attentive ye swains, 'Tis

Phebe invites, and replies to my strains; The

sun never rose on, search all the world through, A

shepherd so bless'd, or a fair one so true, A

shepherd so bless'd, or a fair one so true.

Phebe.

'Tis love, like the sun, that gives light to the year, The

Colin.

'Tis love, like the sun, that gives light to the year, The

H 2 sweetest

Song LI.

Song LI. Come live with me and be my love. Marlow.

The original music.

Come live with me, and be my love, And we will

all the pleasures prove That vallies, groves, or

hills and fields, And all the steepy mountains yields.

A LATER AIR. The editor is in doubt whether there be not a third (exclusive of dr. Arnes scotch air) better than either. It is likewise prettily set as a glee by mr. Webbe.

Come live with me, and be my love, And

we will all the pleasures prove That vallies, groves, or

hills, and fields, And all the steepy mountain yields.

There will we sit up—on the rocks, And

see the shepherds feed their flocks, By shallow rivers,

to whose falls, Me—lodious birds sing madrigals; Me-

lodious birds sing madrigals.

*** To accommodate this tune to the words, a verse must be omitted in the singing.

Song LII. If all the world and love were young. Raleigh.

    May be sung to the same notes.

Song LIII. Where the light cannot pierce, in a grove of tall [trees. Brerewood.
    May be sung to the following air.

Song LIV.

fleeces besprinkled with snow: And the

innocent flocks run for ease to the fold, With their

fleeces besprinkled with snow.

SONG LV. O'er moorlands and mountains, rude, barren, and
[bare. Cunningham.
Set by mr. W. Goodwin.

Affetto.

O'er moorlands and mountains, rude, barren, and

bare, As wilder'd and weary'd I roam; A

gentle young shepherdess sees my de——spair, And

leads

SONG LVI. In the merry month of May. Breton.

Set by dr. Wilson.

side, When as May was in his pride, There I

spy'd all alone, all a-lone, Phil-li—da and Co-ry-don.

SONG LVII. All my pass'd life is mine no more. E. of Ro-
[chester.

Set by dr. John Blow.

All my pass'd life is mine no more, The

fly - - ing hours are gone; Like tran—si—to—ry

dreams giv'n o'er, Whose i———ma—ges are kept in store, By

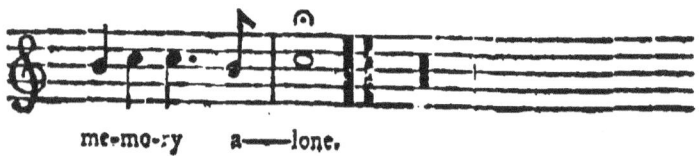

me-mo-ry a———lone.

SONG LVIII.

Song LIX. Though winter its desolate train. Lloyd.

Set by mr. Michael Arne.

Though winter its de—so-late train Of froft and of tempeſt may bring, Yet Flo—ra ſteps for—ward a—gain, And nature revives in the ſpring, re—vives - - Yet Flora ſteps for—ward a—gain, And na—ture revives in the ſpring; And nature revives in the ſpring. Though the

fun

rises with joy in the east, — — And re-

pairs them again in the morn: Yet he

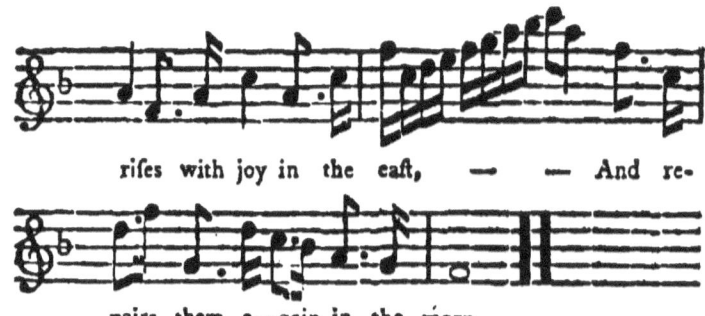
rises with joy in the east, — — And re-

pairs them a—gain in the morn.

SONG LX. When youth, my Celia, 's in the prime. Churchill.

SONG LXI. Behold my fair, where e'er we rove.   Johnson.

SONG LXII. It is not, Celia, in our pow'r.
No airs known.

SONG LXIII. Dear Chloe, while thus beyond measure.

Dear Chloe, while thus, beyond measure, You

treat

treat me with doubts and disdain; You rob all your youth of its pleasure, And hoard up an old age of pain: Your maxim that love is still founded On charms that will quickly decay, You'll find to be very ill grounded, When once you its dictates obey.

Song LXIV. That Jenny's my friend, my delight and my [pride. Moore.

Lively.

That Jenny's my friend, my delight and my pride,

pride, I always have boasted, and seek not to

hide; I dwell on her praises wherever I

go, They say I'm in love, but I answer, no,

no — no, no, no, no, no, no, no, no, no,

no; They say, I'm in love, but I answer, no,

no.

Song LXV. How bless'd has my time been, what days have
[I known. Moore.

Lively.

How bless'd has my time been, what days have I

known,

known, Since wedlocks soft bondage made Jessy my

own! So joyful my heart is, so easy my chain, That

freedom is tasteless and roving a pain; That

freedom is taste—less and roving a pain.

SONG LXVI. In love should there meet a fond pair.
                                             Bickerstaff.
Set by mr. Bernard.

In love should there meet a fond pair, Un-

tutor'd by fashion or art, Whose wishes are warm; are

VOL. I.   I   warm

Song LXVII.

Song LXVII. Away, let nought to love displeasing.
Tune, *Eveillez vous belle endormie.*

Song LXVIII. Ye fair married dames, who so often deplore.
[Garrick.
Set by dr. Arne.

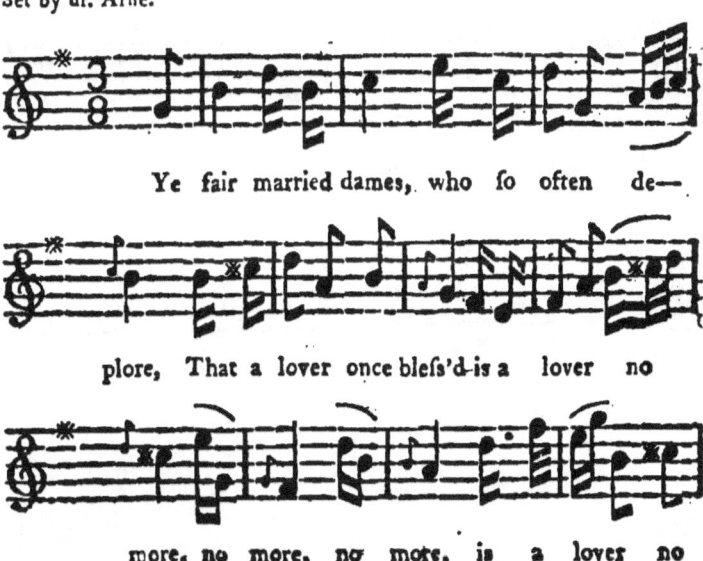

more, At—tend to my counsel, nor blush to be

taught, That prudence must cherish what beauty has

caught: At—tend to my counsel nor blush to be

taught, That pru—dence must che-rish what

beau—ty has caught.

Song LXIX.

SONG LXIX. Ye fair possess'd of ev'ry charm.

Set by dr. Arne.

Song LXX. Say, mighty Love, and teach my song. Watts.

Set by mr. W. Hodson.

cares, To soft——en all their cares.

Song LXXI. Ye belles, and ye flirts, and ye pert little things.
Whitehead.

Ye belles, and ye flirts, and ye pert little things, Who

trip in this fro—lic—some round! Pray tell me from whence this in—de—cen--cy springs, The

sex—es at once to con—found. What means the cock'd hat, and the mas—culine air, With each motion

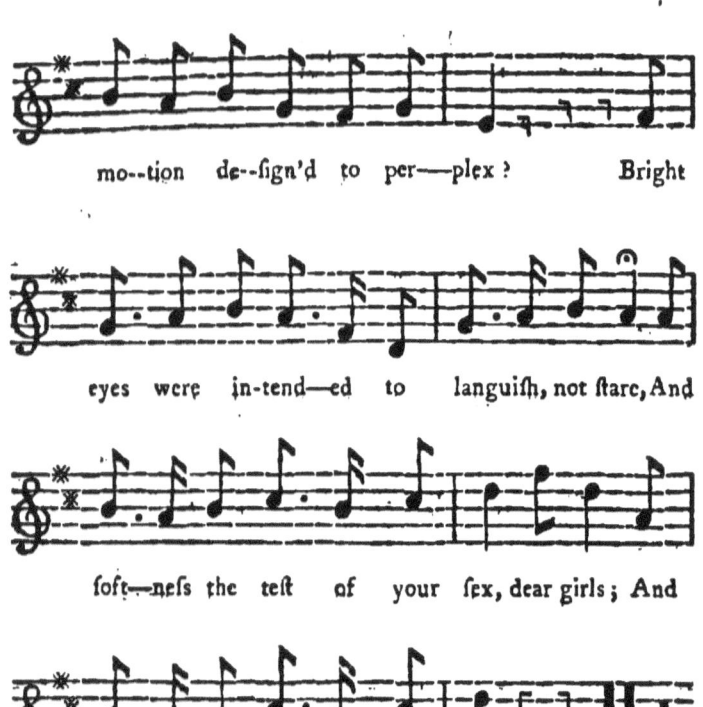

Song LXXII. Child of summer, lovely rose.

No air known.

AIRS
TO THE
SONGS OMITTED.

Ah! stay; ah! turn; ah! whither would you fly? Congreve.

<small>Was originally set by mr. Eccles, and sung by mrs. Hudson. No other air has been discovered.</small>

She, whom above myself I prize.   Carey.

If

If all that I love is her face.

Set by dr. Arne.

Amoroso. If all that I love is her face, From look—ing I sure can re-frain; In o—thers her like—ness may trace, Or ab-sence may cure all my pain. This said, from her charms I re-tir'd, Nor knew I till then how I lov'd;

lov'd; What pre—sent my paf—sion ad——mi..

r'd, In absence my rea—son ap——prov'd.

Think not, my love, when secret grief,

Set by mr. Linley.

Amoroso.

Think not, my love, when se————cret grief Preys on my fad—en'd heart; Think not I wish a mea---n re-lief, Or would from sor-row part;

Or

Send back my long ſtray'd eyes to me.

Ah! cruel maid, how hast thou chang'd.   Sheridan.

The music by mr. Jackson, for Song II. Class V.

⁎ In adapting dr. Parnell's song to the above tune, the following lines (added, it should seem, by the composer,) are to be sung as the concluding verse.

But if she treats me with disdain,
 And slights my well-meant love;
Or looks with pleasure on my pain,
 A pain she won't remove;
Farewell ye birds and lonely pines,
 Adieu to groans and sighs;
I'll leave my passion to the winds,
 Love unreturn'd soon dies.

To melancholy thoughts a prey.   Mrs. Pilkington.

Vol. I.   K   all

all the night to rest: For thee, dis—dain—ful fair, I pine, And wake the ten——der sigh; By that ob——du—rate heart of thine, My balm—y bless—ings fly.

Ye virgin pow'ers defend my heart.

Set by Tho. Farmer, B. M.

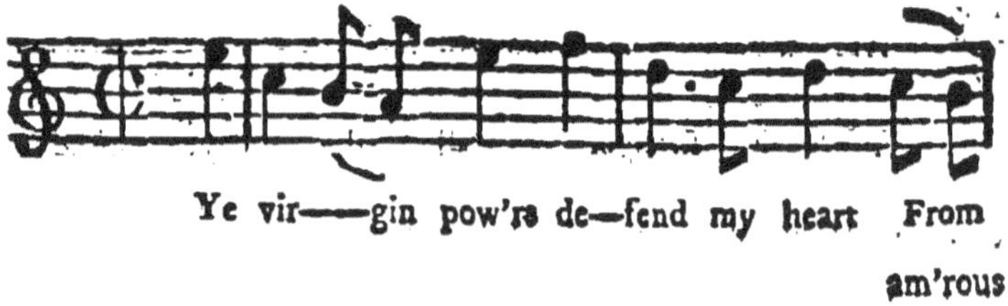

Ye vir——gin pow'rs de—fend my heart From

am'rous

Vain is ev'ry fond endeavour.

Set by dr. Boyce.

Sigh

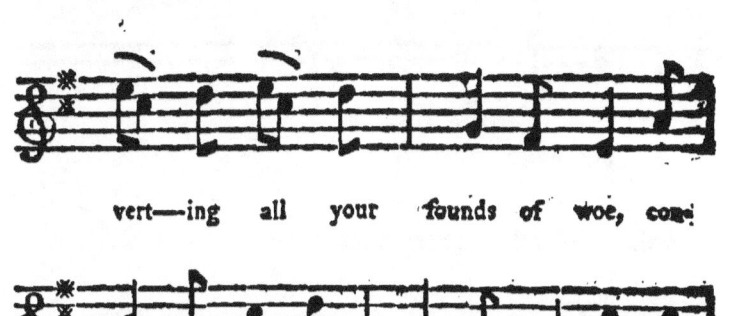

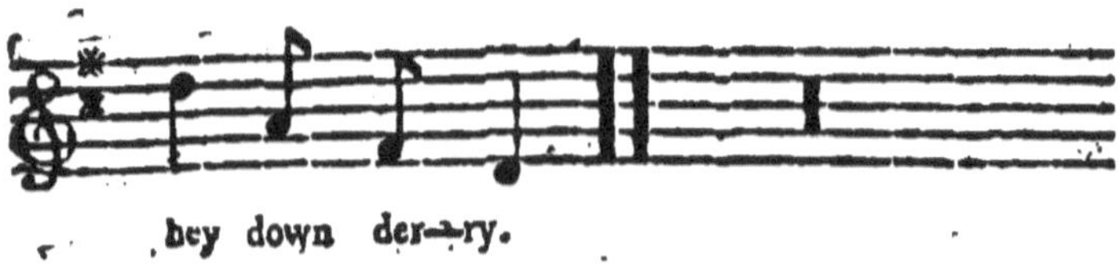
hey down der-ry.

In vain, Philander, at my feet.

Set by dr. Boyce.

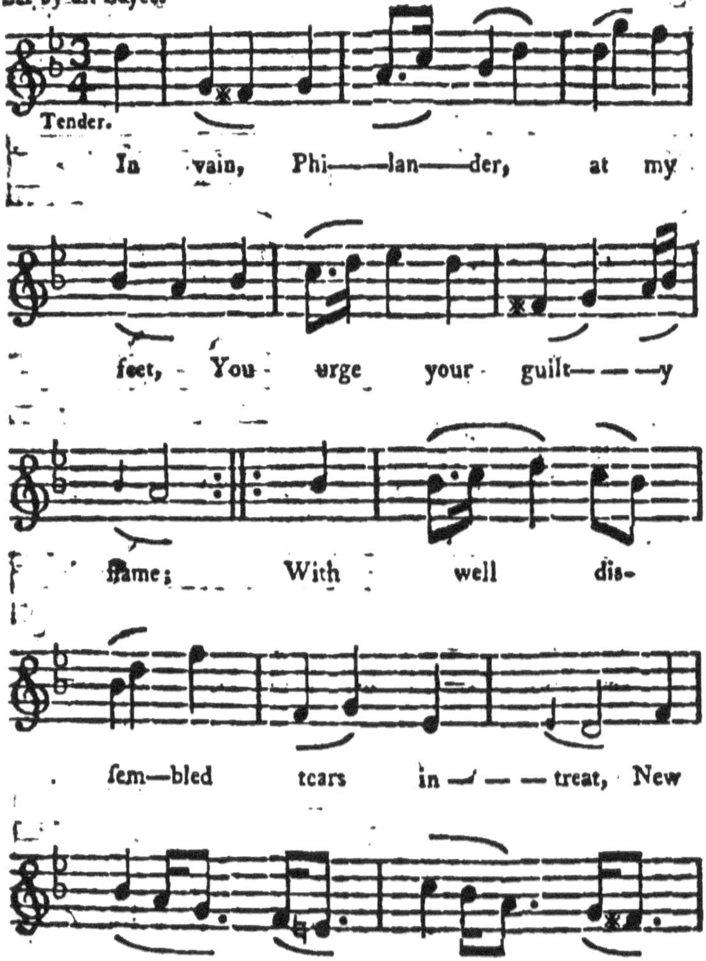
Tender.
In vain, Phi—lan—der, at my
feet, You urge your guilt—y
flame; With well dis-
sem—bled tears in—treat, New
oaths and im—pious

vows

The charms which blooming beauty shows. Fitzgerald.

No air known.

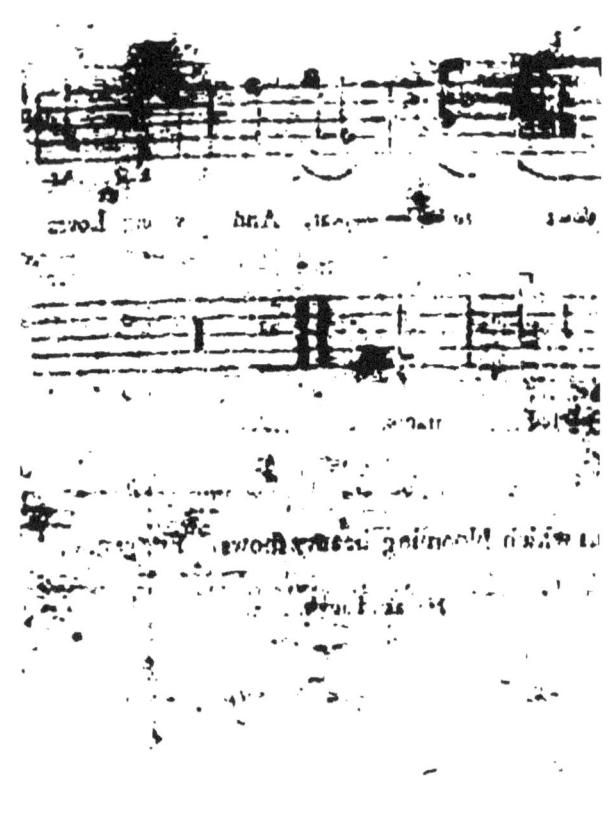

AIRS

TO THE

SONGS

IN

VOLUME II.

A I R S.

PART II.

Song I. Pho! pox of this nonsense, I prythee give o'er.

Pho! pox of this nonsense, I prythee give o'er, And talk of your Phillis and Chloe no more; Their face and their air and their mien, what a rout! Here's to thee my lad, push the bottle about, Here's to thee my lad, to thee my lad, Here's to thee my lad, push the bottle about.

Song II. Better our heads than hearts should ake.
Air unknown.

Song III. Some say women are like the seas.
Set by mr. James Graves.

Song IV.

Song IV. The women all tell me, I'm false to my lass.

The women all tell me I'm false to my lass, That I

quit my poor Chloe and stick to my glass:

But to you men of reason my reasons I'll own; And

if you don't like them why let them alone.

Song V. She tells me with claret she cannot agree.
[D'Urfey?

She tells me with claret she cannot a-

gree, And she thinks of a hogshead when

Song VI.

SONG VI. With an honeſt old friend, and a merry old
[ſong. Carey.

Set by the author.

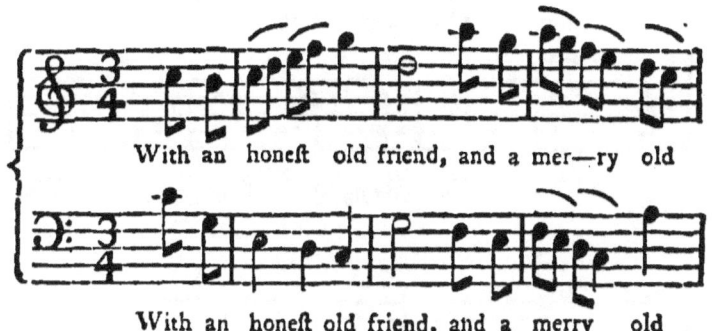

pine

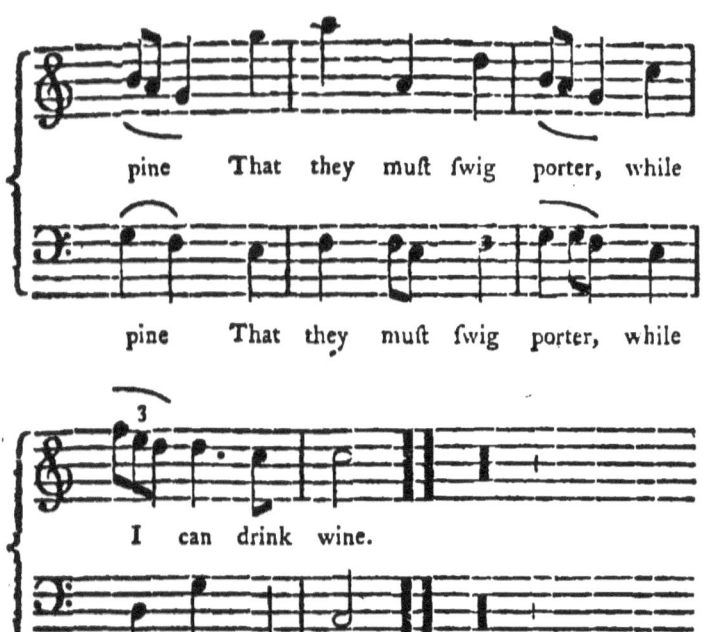

SONG VII. A book, a friend, a song, a glass. Thompson.
No air known.

SONG VIII. Says Plato, why should man be vain. Pilkington.

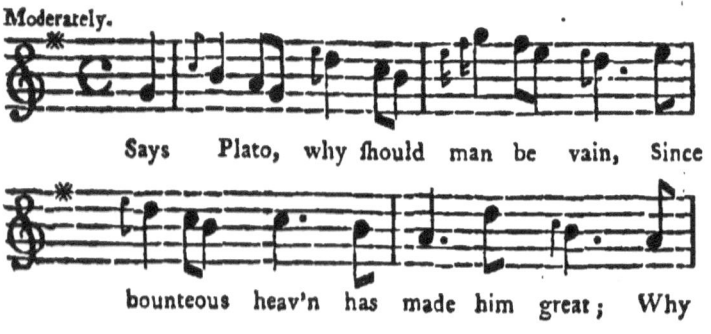

look

look with in-fo—lent difdain, On thofe un-deck'd with

wealth or ftate? Can fplendid robes, or beds of down, Or

coftly gems that deck the fair, Can

all the glo— — — — —

— — — ries of a crown Give

health, or eafe the brow of care?

SONG IX.

Song X. Bid me when forty winters more. Dr. Hill.

Set by dr. Boyce.

Then

Song XI.

Song XI. Youth's the season made for joys. Gay.

Cotilion.

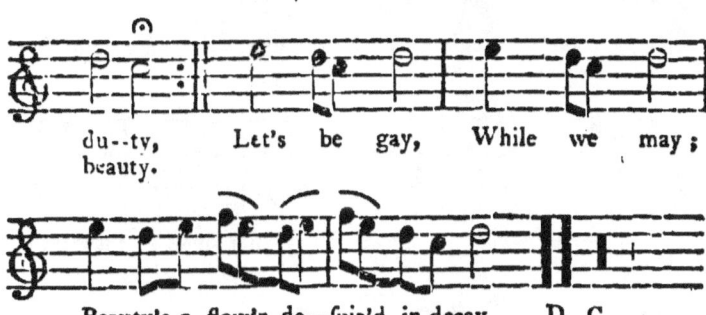

Youth's the season made for joys, Love is then our
She a—lone who that employs, Well deserves her
du--ty, Let's be gay, While we may;
beauty.
Beauty's a flow'r de—spis'd in decay. D. C.

Song XII. Preach not to me your musty rules. Dalton.

Set by dr. Arne.

Piano.

Preach not me your musty rules, Ye drones that
mould in i—dle cell; The heart is wiser
than the schools, The senses always reason
well.

well. If short my span, I less can spare To

pass a single pleasure by; An hour is

long if lost in care, They only live, they only

live, they only live who life enjoy.

Song XIII. Come now, all ye social powers.

Come now, all ye social pow'rs, Shed your influence

o'er us; Crown with joy the present hours, En-

liv—en those be-fore us: Bring the flask, the
music

SONG XIV. What Cato advises most certainly wise is. Carey.
Set by the author.

mingle sweet pleasure, with search after treasure, In-

dulging at night for the toils of the day: And

while the dull miser esteems himself wiser, His

bags to in-crease, while his health does de—cay, Our

souls we enlighten, our fancies we brighten, And

pass the long evenings in pleasure a—way.

Song XV.

Song XV. If gold could lengthen life, I swear.

Set by dr. Worgan.

Then

Song XVI. Let us drink and be merry.

Let us drink and be merry, Dance joke and rejoice, With claret and sherry, The—or—bo and  voice. The changeable world To our joy is unjust. All  treasure's uncertain, Then down with your dust; In  frolics dispose Your pounds, shillings and pence; For  we shall be nothing A hundred years hence.

Song XVII. Jolly mortals fill your glasses.

Jolly mortals fill your glasses, Noble deeds are done

done by wine; Scorn the nymph and all her graces,

Who'd for love or beauty pine. Fa la la la

la la la la la la fa la la la fa la la la

fa la la la la la la la la la fa la la la

la la la.

SONG XVIII. As swift as time put round the glass.

Set by dr. Pepusch.

As swift as time put round the glass, And
husband

husband well lifes little space; Per—haps your sun, which shines so bright, May set in e—ver- last—ing night.

Song XIX. Busy curious thirsty fly.

Set by dr. Green.

Busy, curious, thirsty fly, Drink with me, and
Busy, curious, thirsty fly, Drink with me, and

drink as I; Freely welcome to my cup,
drink as I; Freely welcome to my cup,

could'st

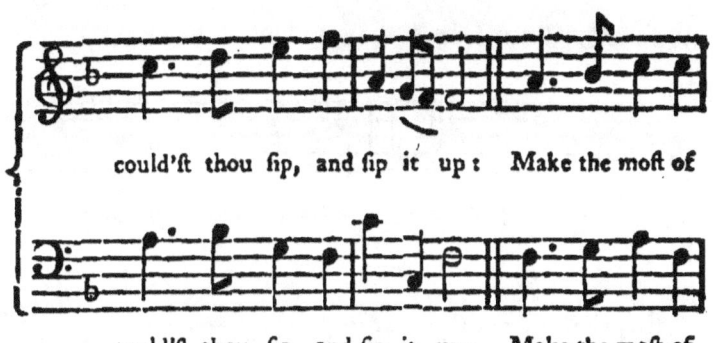

Song XX.

Song XX. When I drain the rosy bowl. Fawkes.

When I drain the ros—y bowl, Joy ex—hi—la-rates my soul; To the Nine I raise my song, E—ver fair and ever young. When full cups my cares dispell, So—ber counsels then farewell: Let the winds, that murmur, sweep All my sorrows to the deep. Let the winds, that mur—mur, sweep All my sor—rows to the deep.

Song XXI.

Song XXI. Mortals, learn your lives to measure.

There is music to this song, but the editor was not able to procure it.

Song XXII. Old Chiron thus preach'd to his pupil Achilles.

Set by mr. Wife.

Old Chi-ron thus preach'd to his pu—pil A-

Old Chi-ron thus preach'd to his

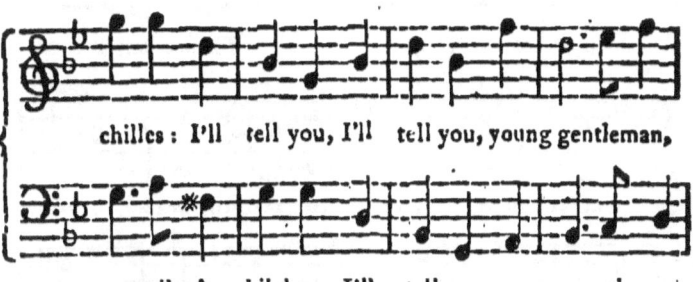

chilles: I'll tell you, I'll tell you, young gentleman,

pu-pil A—chil-les: I'll tell you, young gentleman,

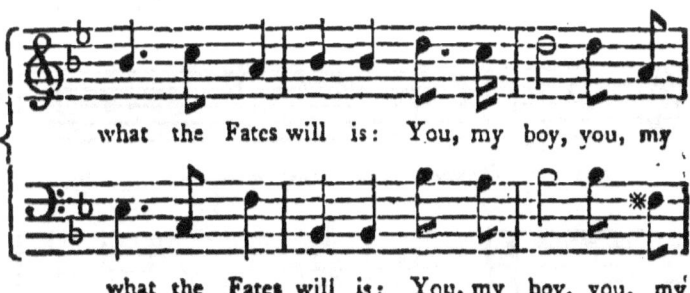

what the Fates will is: You, my boy, you, my

what the Fates will is: You, my boy, you, my

boy,

walls

Song XXIII. Lets be jovial, fill our glasses.

Lets be jovial, fill our glasses, Madness 'tis for

us to think, How the world is rul'd by asses,

And the wise are sway'd by chink. Never let vain

cares op-press us, Riches are to them a snare;

We are all as rich as Cræsus, While our bottle

drowns our care.

Song XXIV.

Song XXIV. Every man take a glass in his hand.

Ev'ry man take a glass in his hand, And drink a good health to the king; Many years may he rule o'er this land, May his laurels for ever fresh spring. Let wrangling and jangling straitway cease, Let ev'ry man strive for his countrys peace; Neither tory nor whig, With their parties look big: Here's a health to all honest men.

Song XXV.

SONG XXV. **Wine, wine in a morning.** Tom Brown.

There are notes to this song, for two voices, by mr. George Hart, in Playfords *Theater of Music*, Book IV. but, like most of the old music, they are so dull and heavy as not to be worth the copying.

SONG XXVI. Had Neptune, when first he took charge of
[the sea.

Set by mr. Ropely.

Had Neptune, when first he took charge of the sea, Been as wise, or at least been as merry as we; He'd have thought better on't, and, instead of his brine, Would have fill'd the vast ocean with ge—nerous wi — — — — — — — ne; Would have fill'd the vast ocean with ge—nerous wine.

SONG XXVII.

Song XXVII. The thirsty earth drinks up the rain. Cowley.

Was originally set by mr. Roger Hill, and is to be found in Playfords second book of *Ayres and Dialogues* by Lawes " and other Excellent Masters." 1669. fol.

Song XXVIII. Ye good fellows all. Dawson.

Ye good fellows all Who love to be told where there's claret good store, At—tend to the call Of one who's ne'er frighted, But greatly delighted With six bottles more. Be sure you don't pass The good house Moneyglass Which the jolly red god so peculiar-ly owns; 'Twill well suit your humour, For pray what would you more Than mirth, with good claret, and bumpers, squire Jones?

C 3

Song XXIX.

Song XXIX. Listen all, I pray. Beaumont.

Song XXX. Come fill me a glass, fill it high.
Airs unknown.

Song XXXI. Rail no more, ye learned asses.
Set by dr. Boyce.

Rail no more, ye learned asses, 'Gainst the

joys the bowl sup—plies; Sound its depth, and fill your

glasses, Wisdom at the bottom lies. Fill them

higher still, and higher, Shallow draughts perplex the

brain; Sip-ing quenches all our fire, Bumpers

light

Song XXXII. Diogenes surly and proud.

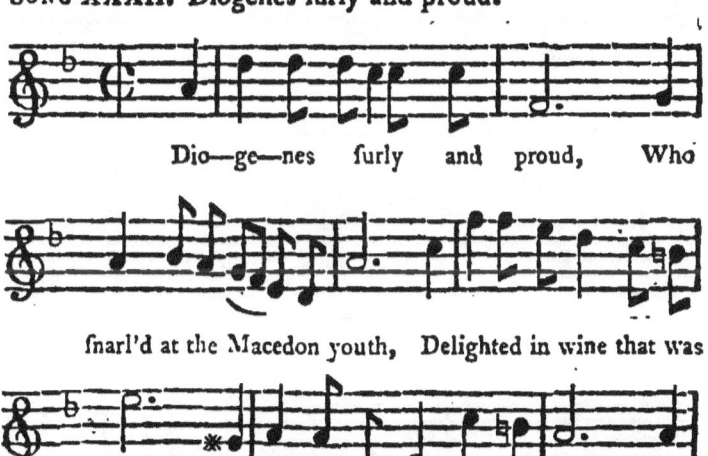

C 4

flask. He chose for his mansion a tub, And liv'd by the scent of the ca — — — — sk, And liv'd by the scent of the cask.

Song XXXIII. Zeno, Plato, Aristotle. Carey.

Set by mr. Lampe.

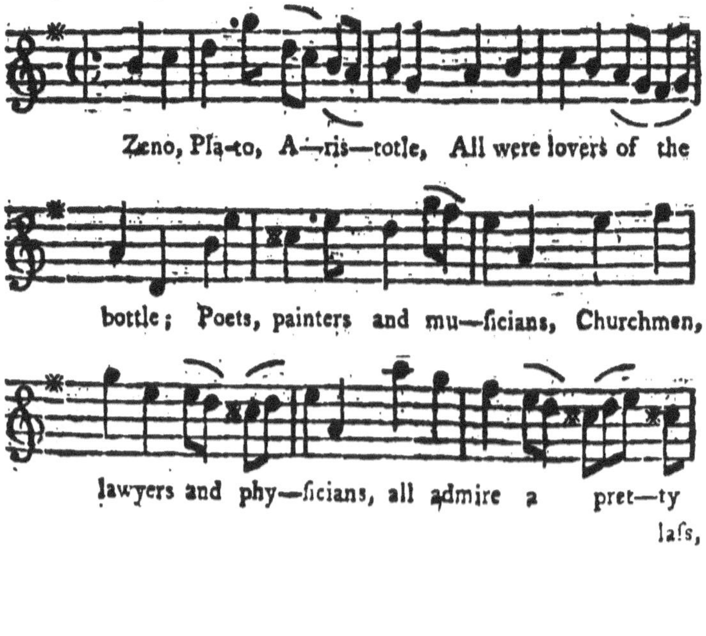

Zeno, Plato, A—ris—totle, All were lovers of the bottle; Poets, painters and mu—sicians, Churchmen, lawyers and phy—sicians, all admire a pret—ty lass,

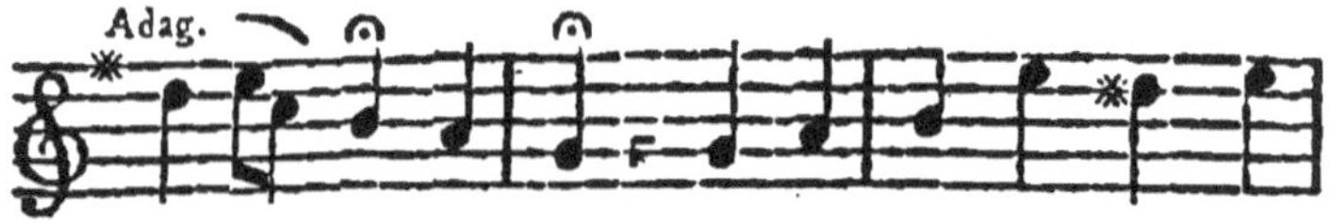

. quire a chearful glaſs. Ev'-ry plea-ſure has its

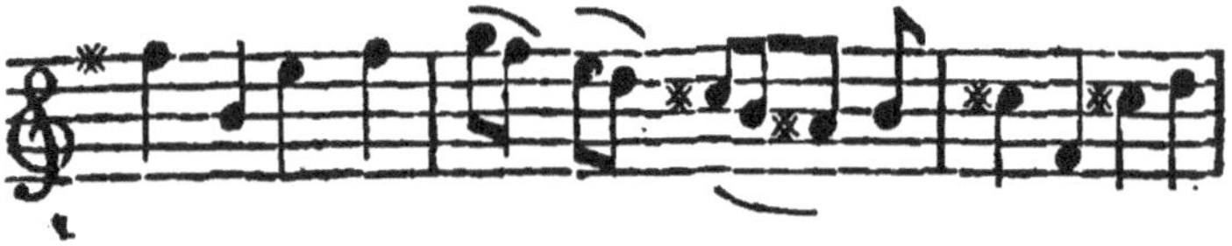

ſeaſon, Love and drink-ing are no treaſon. Ev'ry

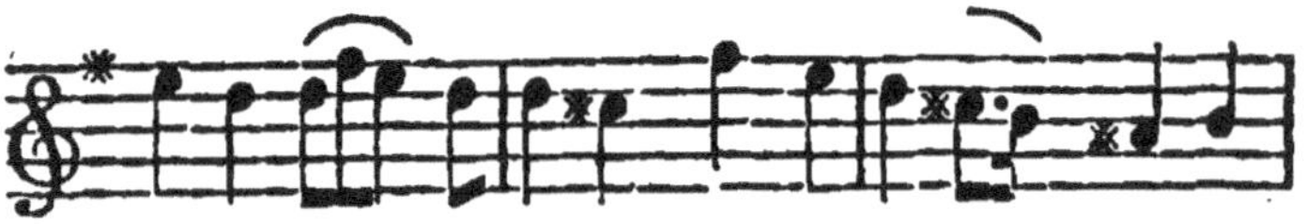

pleaſure has its ſeaſon, Love and drinking are no

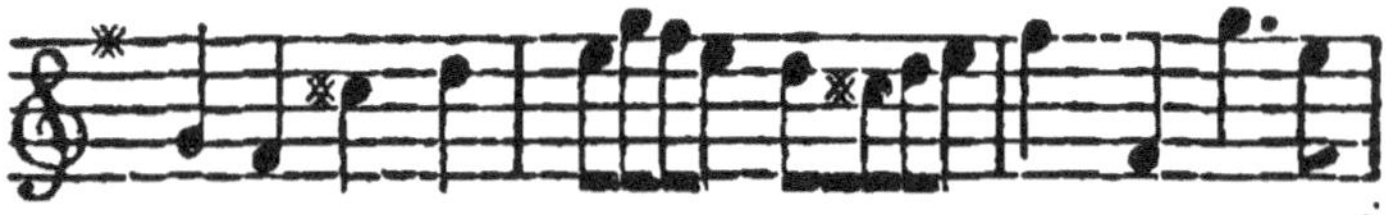

treaſon. Love and drink — — — — — — ing, Love and

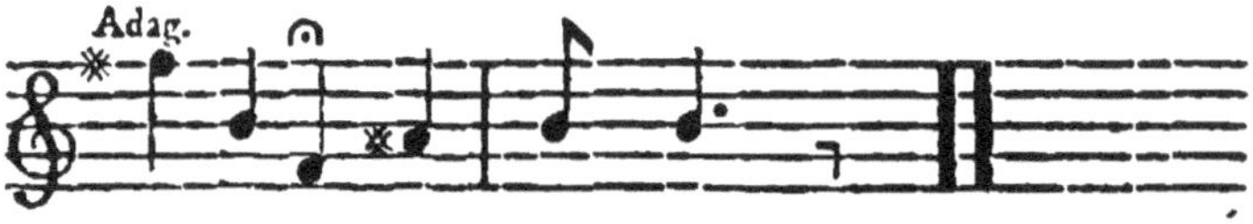

drinking are no trea—ſon. D. C.

SONG XXXIV. Now Phœbus ſinketh in the Weſt. Milton.

Set by dr. Arne.

All°.

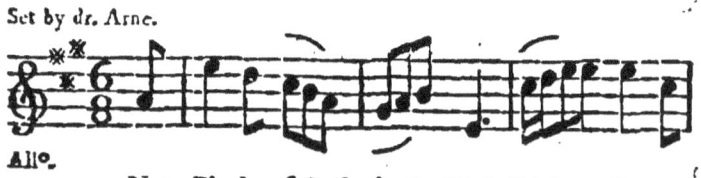

Now Phœbus ſinketh in the Weſt, Welcome ſong and

welcome

flumber

slumber lie With their grave saws in

slumber lie.   D. C.

Song XXXV. By the gayly circling glass.   Dalton.

By the gay-ly cir—cling glass, We can see how

minutes pass: By the hol—low cask are told,

How the waning night grows old. How the waning

night grows old.   Soon too soon the bu—sy day,

Drives

Drives us from our sports a—way; What have we with

day to do, Sons of care 'twas made for you.

Sons of care 'twas made for you.

SONG XXXVI. This bottle's the sun of our table. Sheridan. Set by mr. Linley.

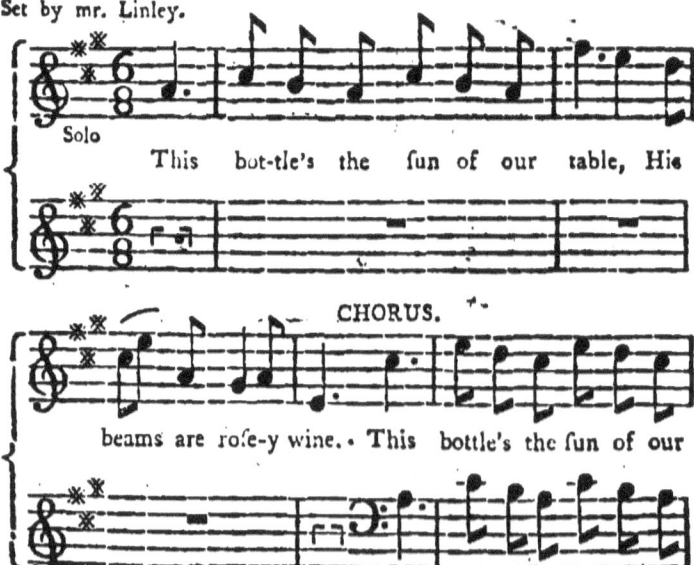

Solo This bottle's the sun of our table, His

CHORUS.
beams are rose-y wine. This bottle's the sun of our

This bottle's the sun of our

table,

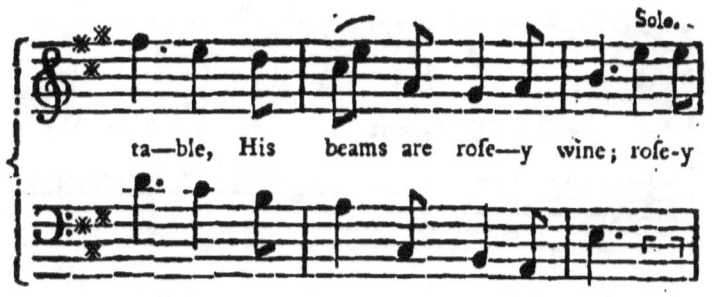
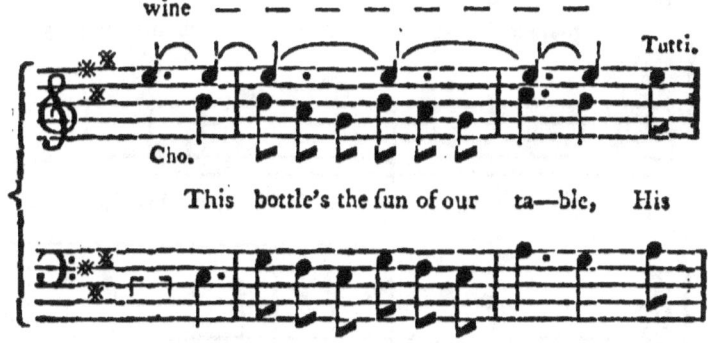
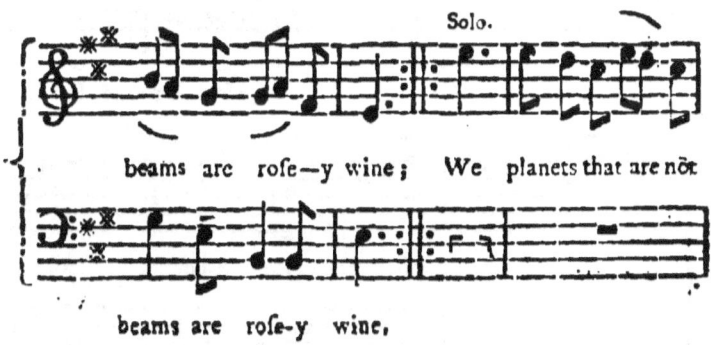

able,

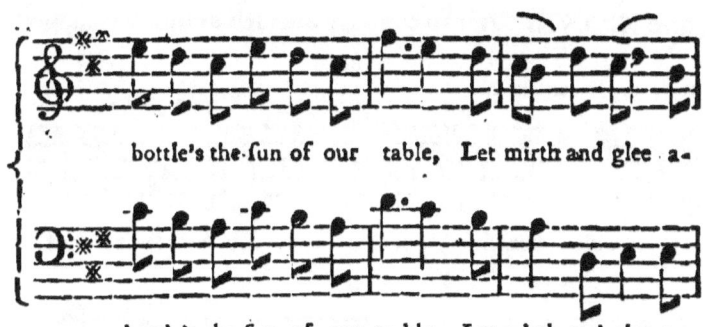

Song XXXVII. Vulcan contrive me such a cup. Rochester.

Set by mr. Fisher Tench.

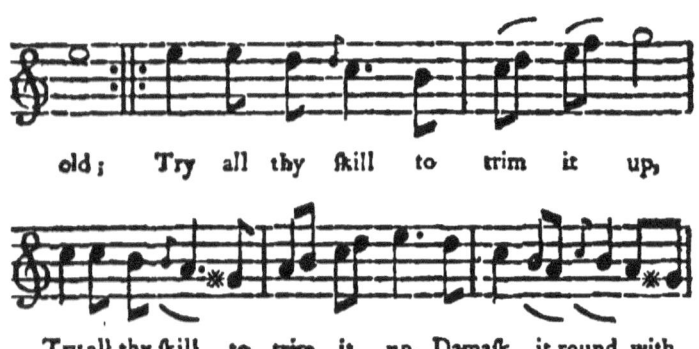

Vulcan contrive me such a cup, As Nes-tor us'd of old; Try all thy skill to trim it up, Try all thy skill to trim it up, Damask it round with gold; Da—mask it round with gold.

Song XXXVIII. Fill me a bowl, a mighty bowl.

Was originally set by dr. Blow, whose composition is much inferior to, and less noticed than the following air by mr. Corfe,

Fill me a bowl, a might—y bowl,

Large

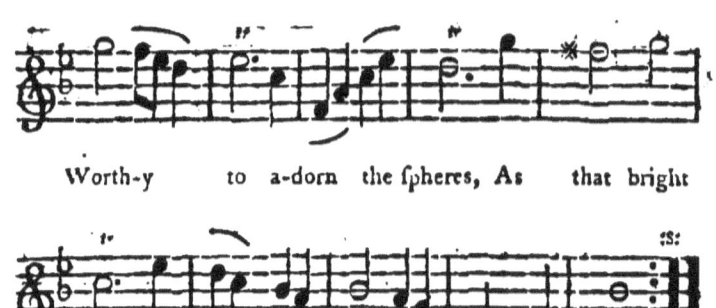

Worth-y to a-dorn the spheres, As that bright cup, as that bright cup a-mongst the stars.

SONG XXXIX. You know that our ancient philosophers hold.

Air unknown.

SONG XL. Let soldiers fight for pay and praise. Johnson.

Let soldiers fight for pay and praise, And money be the mi—sers wish; Poor scholars study all their days, And gluttons glory in their dish.

CHORUS.

'Tis wine, pure wine revives sad souls,

Therefore give me the chear——ing bowls.

SONG XLI. Bacchus must now his power resign. Carey.

Bacchus must now his power resign,

I am the on--ly God of wine, I am the

on--ly God of wine; It is not fit the

wretch should be, In com—pe—ti——tion

Song XLII.

Song XLII. I am the king and prince of drinkers.

man who knows no care, He on-ly deserves the

name of a man.

SONG XLIII. *The man that is drunk is void of all care.*
Tune, *A shepherd kept sheep on a hill so high.*

The man that is drunk is void of all care;
He needs neither Parthi—an qui—ver nor spear;

Fa la la la la la la la la la la: The
Fa la la, &c.

Moors poison'd dart he scorns for to wield; His bottle alone is his

sword and his shield; Fa la la la la la fa la la la la la,

Fa

Fa la la fa la fa fa la la la.

SONG XLIV. Gay Bacchus, liking Eſtcourts wine. Parnell.

Set by mr. Galliard.

Gay Bacchus liking Eſtcourts wine, A no-ble meal be-

ſpoke us; And for the gueſts that were to dine, Brought

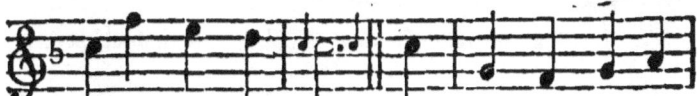

Comus, Love and Jocus. The God near Cu-pid

drew his chair; Near Comus Jo—cus plac'd; For

wine makes love for—get its care, And mirth exalts a

feaſt.

SONG XLV.

Song XLV. **God profper long from being broke.** D. of [Wharton.

Tune *Chevy chafe.* See the laft air of Part III.

Song XLVI. **Come, come my hearts of gold.**

Tune, *Old Sir Simon the king.*

Come, come my hearts of gold, Let us be merry and wife; It

is a proverb of old, Sufpicion hath double eyes:

Whate'er we fay or do, Let's not

drink to difturb the brain; Let's laugh for an hour or two, And

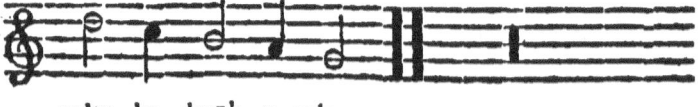

ne'er be drunk a-gain.

Song XLVII.

SONG XLVII. Ye true honest Britons who love your own land.
[Garrick.

Set by dr. Arne.

Ye true honest Britons who love your own land, Whose

fires were so brave, so victo-ri-ous and free, Who

always beat France when they took her in hand, Come

join honest Bri—tons in cho—rus with me.

Join in chorus, in chorus with me; Come join honest Britons in

cho-rus with me. Let us sing our own treasures, Old

Englands

Englands good chear, The profits and pleasures of stout British beer; Your wine-tipling, dram-sip-ing fel-lows retreat, But your beer-drinking Britons can never be beat.

Song XLVIII. When the chill Sirocco blows.

Moderato.

When the chill Si-roc-co blows, And win-ter tells a hea-vy tale; When pyes and daws, and rooks and crows Sit cursing of the

frosts and snows, Then give me ale, Then give me ale,

— then give me ale.

SONG XLIX. Not drunken, nor sober, but neighbour to both.

SONG L. Whilst some in epic strains delight.

Airs unknown.

SONG LI. I cannot eate but lytle meate.

Set, four parts in one, by mr. Walker, before the year 1600.

I cannot eate *my* meate, My stomacke is not

good; But sure I think that I can drynke With

him that weares a hood.

SONG LII.

Song LII. Dear Tom, this brown jug that now foams with
[mild ale. Fawkes.

Set by mr. Hodson.

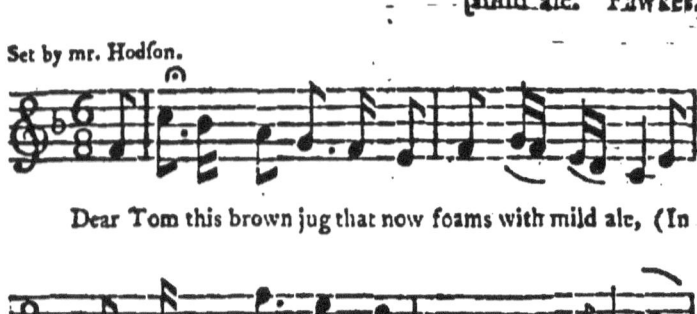

Dear Tom this brown jug that now foams with mild ale, (In

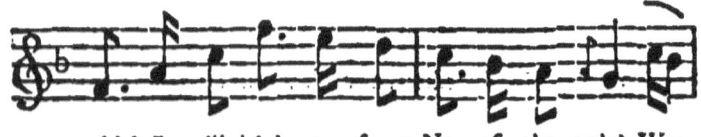

which I will drink to sweet Nan of the vale) Was

once To-by Fill-pot, a thirsty old soul, As

e'er drank a bot-tle or 'fathom'd a bowl. In

bouſ-ing about 'twas his praiſe to excell, And a-

mong jol—ly tope-ers he bore off the bell
bell

bell, He

bore off the bell.

SONG LIII. I have been in love, and in debt, and in drink.
[Brome.
Air unknown.

SONG LIV. Upbraid me not, capricious fair.
Set by mr. Leveridge.

Up-braid me not, ca—pri-cious fair, With

drinking to ex—cefs; I fhould not want to drown de-

fpair, Were your in—diff'rence lefs: Love me my dear and

you

A—ri--adne's coy — — — — — — —

Bacchus only drinks like me, Bacchus only drinks like

me, like me, When A-ri-adne's coy.

Song LV. My temples with clusters of grapes I'll entwine.
[Woty.

Allegro.

My temples with clus—ters of grapes I'll en-

twine, And barter all joys for a gob—let of

wine;

Song LVI.

Song LVI. With women and wine I defy every care. Woty.

Set by mr. Baildon.

With women and wine I de-fy ev'ry care, For

life with-out these is a bubble of air; For

life with-out these, For life without these, For

life without these is a bubble of air. Each

helping the other in plea-sure I roll, And a

new flow of spi-rits en—live—ns my soul. Each

helping

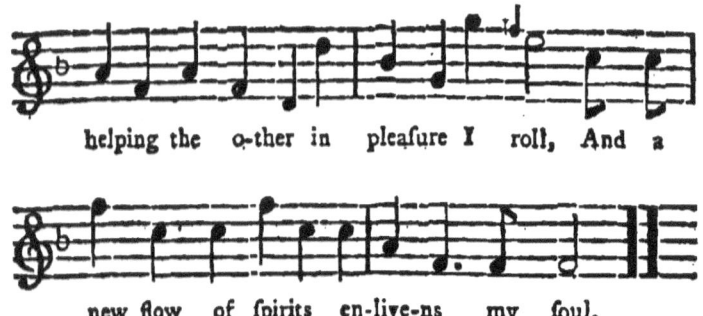

helping the o-ther in pleasure I roll, And a

new flow of spirits en-live-ns my soul.

Song LVII. Adieu, ye jovial youths, who join. Shenstone.

No air known.

A I R S.

Part III.

Song I. My mind to me a kingdom is.

My mind to me a king—dom is; Such

per—fect joy there—in I find, As far excells all

earth—ly bliss That God or Nature hath assign'd.

Though much I want that most would have, Yet

still my mind for——bids to crave.

SONG II. Would we attain the happiest state. Countess of [Winchelsea.

No air known.

SONG III. To hug yourself in perfect ease. Bedingfield.

Set by mr. Dieupart.

To hug yourself in per—fect ease, What would you

wish for more than these? A healthy clean pa-

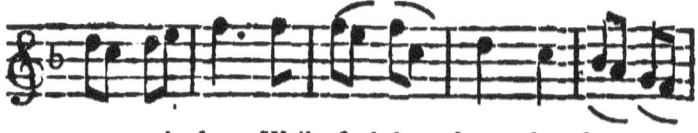

ter—nal seat, Well shaded from the summers

heat.

SONG IV. I envy not the proud their wealth. Mrs. Pilkington.

SONG V. How happy is he born and taught. Wotton.

SONG VI. I envy not the mighty great. Jacob.

No airs known.

SONG VII.

SONG VII. What man, in his wits, had not rather be poor. [Wesley.

Set by mr. Leveridge.

What man, in his wits, had not rather be poor, Than for

lucre his freedom to give? Ever busy the means of his

life to se——cure, And so e——ver neglecting to live;

—— And so e——ver neglect-ing to live.

SONG VIII. No glory I covet, no riches I want. Fitzgerald.

Set by mr. Abiel Whichello.

No glory I covet, no riches I want, Am-

bition is nothing to me; The one thing I beg of kind

Heaven

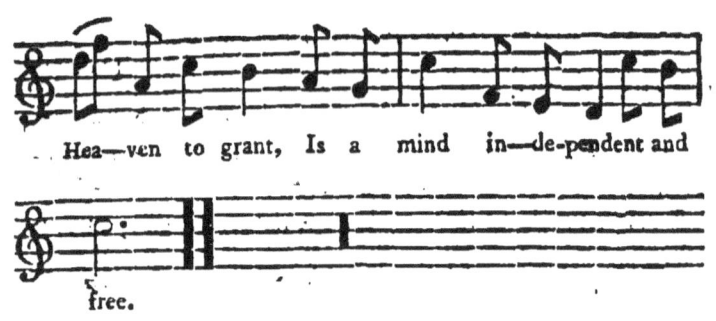

Song IX. Some hoist up fortune to the skies.

No air known.

Song X. The glories of our birth and state. Shirley.

Set by Ed. Coleman. For two voices.

icy

icy hands on Kings: Scepter and crown Must tumble down, And in the dust be e—qual made, With the poor crooked scythe and spade.

SONG XI. Nor on beds of fading flowers. Dalton.

Set by dr. Arne.

Nor on beds of fade—ing flow'rs, Shed-ing

soon

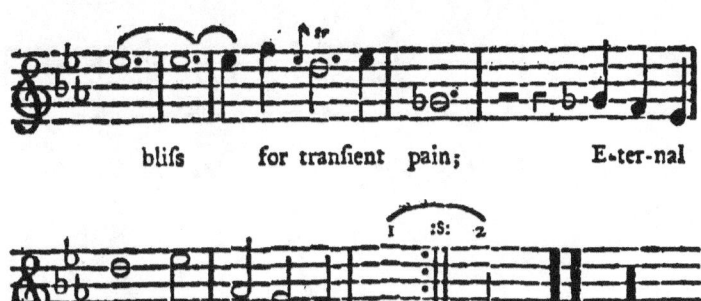

bliss for transient pain; E-ter-nal

bliss for tran—sient pain.

SONG XII. What frenzy must his soul possess. Hoole.

SONG XIII. To tinkling brooks, to twilight shades. Warton.

No airs known.

SONG XIV. Come, come, my good shepherds, our flocks [we must shear. Garrick.

Set by mr. Michael Arne.

Come, come, my good shepherds, our flocks we must shear,

In your ho-li-day suits with your lass-es appear; The

happiest of folk are the guile-less and free, And

who

Song XV. How sacred and how innocent. Mrs. Philips.

Song XVI. Through groves sequester'd, dark and still.
[Hawkesworth.

No airs known.

Song XVII.

Song XVII. Goddess of ease leave Lethes brink. Smart.

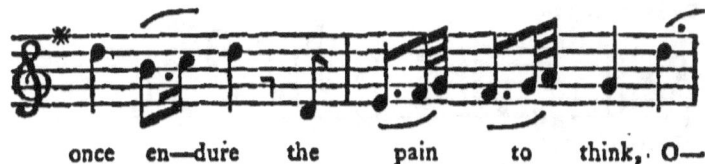

sweet—ly thought—less let them flow;

sweet—ly thoughtless let them flow.

Song XVIII. From the court to the cottage convey me away.
[Carey.

Set by the author.

Moderato.

From the court to the cottage con—vey me a-

way, For I'm wea-ry of grandeur and what they call

gay; From the court to the cottage con-vey me a-

way, For I'm wea-ry of grandeur and what they call

gay:

gay: Where pride with-out mea-fure and

pomp without pleafure, Make life in a cir-cle of

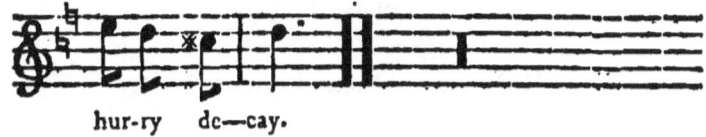

hur-ry de-cay.

SONG XIX. Princes that rule and empire fway. Otway.

SONG XX. What is th' exiftence of mans life, Bp. King.

SONG XXI. The fweet and blufhing rofe. Lillo.

SONG XXII. Man's a poor deluded bubble. Dodfley.

No airs known.

SONG XLIX. O fay what is that thing call'd light. Cibber.

Set by mr. Stanley.

O fay, what is that thing call'd light, Which

I can ne'er en- -joy? What are the

bleffings

bless——ings of the sight? O tell, tell your poor blind boy.

SONG XXIV. Welcome, welcome brother debtor. Coffey.

Welcome, wel——come, bro-ther debtor, To this

poor but merry place; Where no bai——lif, dun, or

setter Dare to show his frightful face. But, kind

sir, as you're a stranger, Down your garnish you must

lay;

lay; Or your coat will be in danger, You must

The last line is usually sung thus.

ei—ther strip or pay.   You must

ei—ther strip or pay.

Song XXV. How pleasant a sailors life passes.

How pleasant a sailors life passes, Who

roams o'er the wa—tery main; No treasure he e—ver a-

masses, But chearfully spends all his gain.

Song XXVI. How happy a state does the miller possess.
[Highmore.

How happy a state does the miller possess, Who

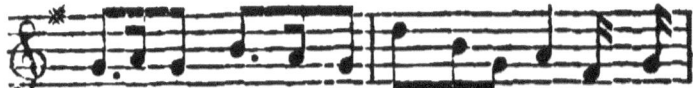

would be no greater, nor fears to be less; On his

mill and himself he depends for support, Which is

better than servilely cringing at court. What tho' he all dusty and

whiten'd does go, The more he's be—powder'd the

more like a beau: A clown in this dress may be

ho-nester far Than a courtier who struts in his

garter

garter and ſtar; Than a courtier who ſtruts in his

gar—ter and ſtar.

SONG XXVII. The honeſt heart whoſe thoughts are clear.
[Bickerſtaff.

Set to a tune of Mr. Feſting.

The ho—neſt heart whoſe thoughts are clear From

fraud diſguiſe and guile, Need nei—ther Fortunes

frowning fear, Nor court the har—lots ſmile: The

greatneſs that would make us grave Is but an emp—ty,

empty

emp-ty thing; What more than mirth would mortals have? What

more than mirth would mor-tals have? The chearful, chearful

man's a king, The chearful man's a king.

SONG XXVIII. If I live to grow old, as I find I go down. Pope.

Set by dr. Blow.

If I live to grow old, as I find I go

down, Let this be my fate in a coun—try

town; May I have a warm house with a stone at my

gate, And a cleanly young girl to rub my bald pate;

CHORUS.

May I go-vern my paſſion with an ab—ſo—lute

ſway, And grow wiſer and better as my ſtrength wears a—

way, Without gout or ſtone, Without gout or ſtone by a

gentle de—cay, by a gen— — — — —

— —tle de—cay.

Song XXIX. The solitary bird of night. Miss Carter.

Set by Miss *CLARISSA HARLOWE*.

The so—li—ta—ry bird of night

Through the thick shades now wings his flight, And

quits his time-shook tow'r; And quits his time-shook

tow'r; Where, shelter'd from the blaze of day, In

phi--lo-sophic gloom he lay, Beneath his i——vy

bow'r; Beneath his i—vy bow'r.

Song XXX.

Song **XXX.** Friendship peculiar gift of heaven.   Mrs. [Williams.

No air known.

Song **XXXI.** The world, my dear Myra, is full of deceit.

Set by mr. John Gerrard.

Moderately brisk.   The world my dear My-ra is full of de-

ceit, And friendship's a jew-el we seldom can

meet; How strange does it seem, that, in searching a-

round, This source of content is so rare to be

found. O friendship, thou balm, and rich

sweet-

sweet'ner of life, Kind parent of ease and com-

pos-er of strife, With—out thee, a—las! what are

riches and pow'r? But emp—ty de—lu—sion, the

joys of an hour — — —; But

emp—ty de—lu—sion, the joys of an hour.

SONG XXXII. Blow, blow, thou winter wind. Shakspeare.
Set by dr. Arne.

Gently.

Blow, blow, thou winter wind, Thou art not so un-

kind

Song XXXIII.

Song XXXIII. Go foul, the bodys gueſt.   Daviſon.
Air unknown.

Song XXXIV. When this old cap was new.
"To the tune of, Ile nere be drunk againe."

Song XXXV. In good king Charleſes golden days.

In good king Charleſes golden days, When

loyalty no harm meant, A zealous high-church-

man I was, And ſo I got pre—ferment. To

teach my flock I ne-ver miſt Kings were by God ap-

pointed! And damn'd are thoſe that do reſiſt, Or

touch

CHORUS.

touch The Lords A—nointed: And this is law I

will maintain, Un—till my dy-ing day, sir, That

whatso—ever king shall reign, I'll be the Vicar of

Bray, sir.

Song XXXVI. Cease rude Boreas, blust'ring railer! Stevens.
    See the Music to Song LXIV. in this part.

Song XXXVII. You gentlemen of England.

You gentlemen of England, Who live at home at

ease, How little do you think upon The dangers of the

seas

feas : Give ear unto the ma-ri-ners, And they will plainly

fhow, All the cares, and the fears, When the

CHORUS.

ftormy winds do blow: All the cares, and the

fears, When the ftormy winds do blow.

Song XXXVIII. The wretch condemn'd with life to part,
[Goldfmith.

Set by mr. Hook.

The wretch condemn'd with life to part, Yet,

yet on hope re——lies : And ev'ry pang that

rends

ta—pers light, A-dorns and chears our way; And

still, as dark-er grows the night, E—

mits a brighter ray; E—mits a bright-er

ray; E—-mits a brighter ray.

SONG XXXIX. O memory! thou fond deceiver. Goldsmith.
Air unknown.

SONG XL. Gently stir and blow the fire.
Signor Geminiani's minuet.

Gen—tly stir and blow the fire,

the

Lay the mutton down to roast; Dress it quick--ly I de—sire, In the dripping put a toast, That I hun——ger may re—move, Mut—ton is the meat I love.

Song XLI. When Orpheus went down to the regions below. [Lisle.

Set by dr. Boyce.

When Orpheus went down to the regions below, Which

men

SONG XLII

SONG XLII. Two gossips they merryly met.

Two gossips they merry—ly met, At

nine in the morning full soon; And they were resolv'd for a

whet, To keep their sweet voices in tune; A-

way to the tavern they went; Here, Joan, I do vow and pro-

test, That I have a crown yet un-spent; Come,

let's have a cup of the best.

Song XLIII. With an old song, made by an old ancient pate.

With an old song, made by an old ancient pate, Of an old wor—ship—full gen—tle—man, who had a great estate, Who kept an old house at a boun—ty—full rate, And an old porter to re—lieve the poor at his gate: Like an old courtier of the queens, And the queens old courtier.

Song XLIV.

Song XLIV. When daffodils begins to peer. Shakſpeare.

This tune is not known to have been ever printed before, and was not obtained without ſome difficulty. The two laſt verſes were transpoſed in the copy, but are here placed in their proper order.

When daf—fodils be—gin to peer, With, hey! the doxy

o—ver the dale! Why then comes in the

ſweet o' the year, For the red blood reigns in the

winters pale. The white ſheet bleaching

on the hedge, With, hey! the ſweet birds, how they ſing! Doth

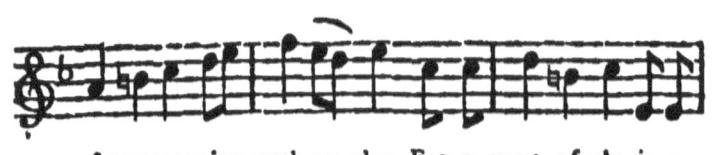

tirra

SONG XLV. When daysies pied, and violets blue. Shakſpeare.

Set by dr. Arne.

Allegro non troppo.

When daysies pied, and violets blue, And

lady-ſmocks all ſi!ver white, And cuckow-buds of

yellow hue, Do paint the meadows with delight, The

cuckow, then, on ev'ry tree, Mocks marry'd men,

mocks marry'd men, mocks marry'd men, for thus ſings he:

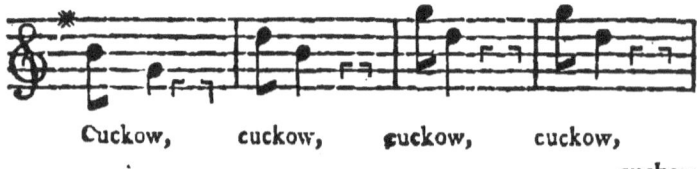

Cuckow, cuckow, cuckow, cuckow,

cuckow,

cuckow, cuckow; — o word of fear! o word of fear! Un—pleasing to a marry'd ear, Un—pleasing to a marry'd ear.

SONG XLVI. When icicles hang on the wall. Shakspears.

Set by dr. Arne.

Poco allegro.

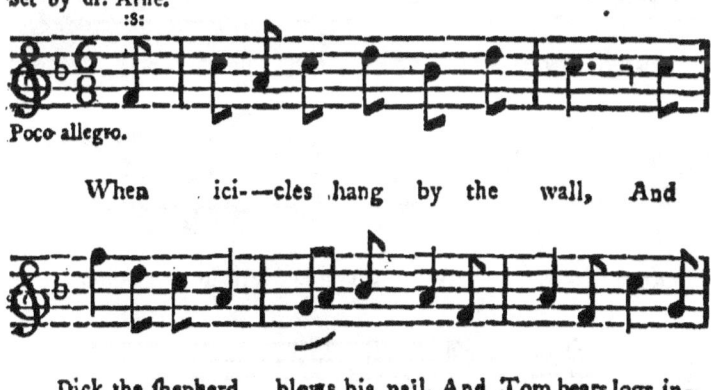

When ici—cles hang by the wall, And Dick the shepherd blows his nail, And Tom bears logs in-

Song XLVII. Under the green-wood tree. Shakſpeare.

Set by dr. Arne.

Non troppo allegro.

Under the green-wood tree, Who loves to lye with

me, And tune his merry note, his

merry, merry note, Unto the ſweet birds throat; And

tune his merry note, Un——to the ſweet birds

throat; Come hither, hither, come

hither, come hither, come hither, come

hither,

Song XLVIII.

SONG XLVIII. Forth from my dark and dismal cell.

Set by mr. Purcell.

Forth from my dark and dismal cell, Or from the deep a-

byss of hell, Mad Tom is come to view the world again, To

see if he can cure his distemper'd brain. Fears and cares op-

press my soul, Hark! how the an—gry Furies howl:

Pluto laughs, and Pro-fer—pine is glad, To

see poor an—gry Tom of Bed—lam mad.

Through

SONG XLIX. Come, shepherds, let's follow the hearse.
[Cunningham.

No air of merit has been met with. But *quære* if it were not set by dr. Alcock of Litchfield?

SONG L. Sleep, sleep, poor youth, sleep, sleep in peace.
D'Urfey.

This air has not been found.

SONG LI. How sleep the brave, who sink to rest. Collins.

Has only been set as a glee.

SONG LII.

Song LII. To fair Fideles grafsy tomb.   Collins.

Set by dr. Arne.

Song LIII. Thou foft flowing Avon, by thy filver ftream.
[Garrick.

Set by dr. Arne.

Larghetto.

things

things more than mortal thy Shakſpeare would dream, would

dream, would dream, thy Shakſpeare would dream: The

Fairies, by moonlight, dance round the green bed, For

hallow'd the turf is which pil-low'd his head: The

Fairies, by moonlight, dance round the green bed, For

hallow'd the turf is which pil—low'd his

head.

SONG LIV.

Song LIV. Oft i've implor'd the gods in vain. Mrs. Greville.

Has been set as a Cantata.

Song LV. Come, follow, follow me.

Come, follow, follow me, Ye Fairy Elves that

be Light trip-ing o'er the green; Come

follow Mab your queen: Hand in hand we'll dance around,

For this place is Fairy ground,

Song LVI. Lo! here, beneath this hallow'd shade.

No air known.

Song LVII. From Oberon, in Fairy-land.

"Tune is, *Dulina*." *

From Oberon, in Fairy land, The king of ghosts and shadows there, Mad Robin I, at his command, Am sent to view the night sports here; What revel rout is kept about, In every corner where I go, I will o'erfee, and merry be, And make good sport, with ho! ho! ho!

Song LVIII.

* This Song, which is very old, may be seen in Percys collection.

SONG LVIII. Happy insect, what can be. Cowley.

No air known, worth inserting.

SONG LIX. Songs of shepherds, in rustical roundelays.

Songs of shepherds, in rustical roundelays,

Form'd in fancy, and whistled on reeds, Sung to solace young

nymphs upon holydays, Are too un—worth-y for

wonderfull deeds. Sot-ish Silenus To Phœbus the genius Was

sent by dame Venus, a song to prepare, In phrase nicely coin'd,

And verse quite refin'd, How the states divine

hunted the hare.

SONG LX. Hark! hark! jolly sportsmen, a while to my tale.

Hark! hark! jol-ly sportsmen, a while to my tale, To

pay your attention I'm sure it cann't fail: 'Tis of

lads,

lads, and of horses, and dogs that ne'er tire, O'er

stone walls and hedges, thro' dale, bog and briar: A

pack of such hounds, and a set of such men, 'Tis a

shrewd chance if ever you meet with again; Had

Nimrod, the mightyest of hunters, been there,'Fore

gad he had shook like an as——pen, for fear.

Song LXI.

Song LXI. Who has e'er been at Paris must needs know the
[*Grève*. Prior.

Who has e'er been at Pa—ris must

needs know the *Grève*, The fa———tal re-treat of th'un-

for—tu-nate brave; Where ho——nour and justice moſt

odd—ly con-tribute To eaſe heroes pains by a

hal—ter and gib—bet. Der——ry down, down,

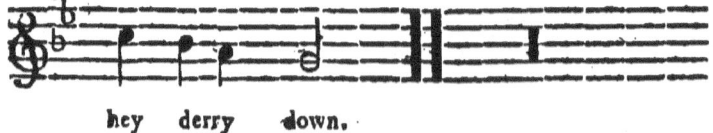

hey derry down.

Song LXII.

Song LXII. In Tyburn-road a man there liv'd.

May be sung to the *Children in the wood*, (See the music, Part I. Class III. Song XLI.)

Song LXIII. As near Porto Bello lying. Glover.

As near Por-to Bello ly—ing On the gently swelling

flood, At mid—night, with streamers flying, Our tri-

umphant navy rode; There, while Ver-non fate all-

glorious From the Spaniards late de—feat, And his

H 4   crews,

crews, with shouts vic———-to—ri-ous, Drank suc-

cess to Englands fleet.

Song LXIV. The muse and the hero together are fir'd.

Set by mr. Oswald.

The muse and the hero together are fir'd, The

same noble views have their bo—soms in—spir'd; As

free—dom they love, and for glory con-tend, The

muse

muse o'er the he—ro still mourns as a friend; And

here let the muse her poor tri——bute bequeath To

one Brit—ish he—ro, 'tis brave cap-tain Death; 'Tis

brave cap-tain Death, 'tis brave captain Death; To

one British he—ro, 'tis brave captain Death.

Song LXV.

Song LXV. Thursday in the morn, the ides of May.

every

every hand supply his gun; Follow me, And you'll

see That the bat—tle will be soon be-gun: Fol-low

me, And you'll see That the battle will be soon be—

gun.

AIRS.

AIRS.

PART IV.

BALLAD I. Lord Thomas he was a bold forestèr.
  " To a pleasant tune called, *Lord Thomas*, &c."

BALLAD II. As it fell out upon a day.
  The notes of the tune or tunes to these two ballads have not been discovered.

BALLAD III. You dainty dames so finely fram'd.
  " To the tune of, *The Lady's Fall.* " See below.

BALLAD IV. When Troy town, for ten years wars.

When Troy town, for ten years wars, With-

stood the Greeks in man———ful wise,

Then

Then did their foes en——creafe fo faft, That

to re—fift none could fuf——fice:

Wafte lie thofe walls, that were fo good, And

corn now grows where Troy town ftood.

BALLAD V. Will you hear a Spanifh lady.

"To a pleafant new tune." Not known.

BALLAD VI. Mark well my heavy doleful tale.

"To the tune of, *In Pefcod time*, &c." This is prefumed to be the fame air with that of the *Children in the Wood*.

BALLAD VII.

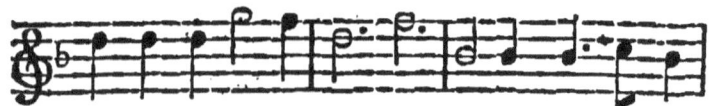

met with a farmers daughter; Rof-y cheeks and a

bonny brow; Good faith, my mouth did

wa—ter.

BALLAD XVIII. When Arthur first in court began.

"To the tune of *Flying Fame*." The same with *Chevy Chafe*, and a moft favourite melody with the old ballad makers. See the laft air of this part.

BALLAD XIX. Was ever knight for ladys fake.

"Tune, *Was ever man*, &c."

BALLAD XX. Of a worthy London prentice.

"To the tune of, *All you that love good fellows*, &c."

Of a worthy Lon—don pren—tice My

purpofe

purpose is to speak, And of his brave ad-

ventures Done for his coun—trys sake:

Seek all the world a——bout, And

you shall hardly find A man in va—lour

to exceed A prentice' gallant mind.

BALLAD XXI. Old stories tell how Hercules.

Old sto—ries tell, how Her—cules A

dragon flew at Lerna, With se—ven heads and

four—teen eyes, To see and well dis-

cern—a; But he had a club This

dragon to drub, Or he had ne'er done't, I

warr'nt

BALDAD XXII. When Flora with her fragrant flowers.

"To the tune of, *Come follow my Love*."

BALLAD XXIII. Is there never a man in all Scotland.

"To a pretty new Northern tune."

BALLAD XXIV.

BALLAD XXIV. God prosper long our noble king.

"Tune, Flying Fame."

God prosper long our noble king, Our lives and safeties

all, A woefull hunting once there did In Chevy-chase be-

fall.

AIRS.

AIRS,
TO THE
SONGS OMITTED,
IN PART II.

Cupid no more shall give me grief. Carey.

Set by the author.

How

How stands the glass around.

How stands the glass around? For shame, ye take no

care, my boys; How stands the glass a-round? Let

mirth and wine a——bound. The trumpets

sound: The colours flying are, my boys, To

fight, kill or wound: May we still be found Con-

tent with our hard fare, my boys, On the cold

ground.

The festive board was met, the social band.

The festive board was met, the social

band, Round fam'd A—na--creon took their si—lent

stand: My sons, (began the sage) be this the rule:

No brow austere must dare ap-proach my school:

Where Love and Bacchus jointly reign with—

in, Old Care, be gone! Old Care, be gone! here

sadness

gives soft wishes birth, And Bacchus, god of wine and

mirth, Me their friend and fav'rite own, Me their

friend and fav'rite own, And I was born for them a—lone:

I was born — — — — —

— for them a—lone. I was born for them a—lone.

Bus'ness, title, title, pomp and state,

Title

ncing

— ncing, Speed the dancing hours a—way;.

Mind not what the grave ones say;

Mind not, mind not what the grave ones

say.

When Bacchus, jolly god invites. Whitehead.
  Has been set: But the only composition met with was a very indifferent cantata.

Hence with cares, complaints and frowning. Bickerstaff.
  Was set to the air of Song XXXI. Part II. See the Music.

INDEX.

VOLUME I.

PART I.

(LOVE SONGS.)

N. B. The songs and ballads marked in these indexes with an asterism are those of which the different volumes contain the musical airs.

	Page
* A COBLER there was, and he liv'd in a stall	154
* A courting I went to my love	146
A maxim this, amongst the wise	97
Ah! blame me not, if no despair	17
Ah, Chloris! could I now but sit	1
* Ah! cruel maid, how hast thou chang'd	258
* Ah, Damon, dear shepherd, adieu	70
* Ah, false Amyntas! can that hour	167
* Ah! gaze not on those eyes! forbear	5
* Ah! how sweet it is to love	89
Ah! stay; ah! turn; ah! whither would you fly	255
* Ah! why must words my flame reveal	161
* Alexis shunn'd his fellow swains	75

Vol. II.   * K   * All

INDEX.

* All in the Downs the fleet was moor'd	214
* All my paſt life is mine no more	236
* Almerias face, her ſhape, her air	4
* As Amoret with Phillis ſat	157
As he lay in the plain, his arm under his head	176
* Aſk me not how calmly I	88
* Away! let nought to love diſpleaſing	246
* Away with theſe ſelf-loving lads	120
* BE ſtill, o ye winds, and attentive, ye ſwains	226
Behold, my fair, wheree'er we rove	240
Belinda, ſee from yonder flow'rs	111
* Bleſs'd as th' immortal gods is he	188
* Boaſt not, miſtaken ſwain, thy art	165
* By my ſighs you may diſcover	261
* CAN love be controul'd by advice	237
Ceaſe to blame my melancholy	186
Child of ſummer, lovely Roſe	253
Chloris, 'twill be for eithers reſt	121
* Come all ye youths whoſe hearts e'er bled	66
* Come, Chloe, and give me ſweet kiſſes	202
* Come, dear Amanda, quit the town	223
Come, dear Paſtora, come away!	220
Come here, fond youth, whoe'er thou be	95
Come let us now reſolve at laſt	118
Come liſten to my mournful tale	81
* Come live with me, and be my love	228
* Come thou roſy-dimpled boy	87
Could you gueſs, for I ill can repeat	28

DEAR

INDEX.

D EAR Chloe, how blubber'd is that pretty face	136
* Dear Chloe, while thus beyond measure	242
* Dear Colin, prevent my warm blushes	159
Dejected as true converts die	177
* Despairing beside a clear stream	64
Distracted with care	148
F AIN would you ease my troubled heart	15
* Fair Iris I love, and hourly I die	122
* Fairest isle, all isles excelling	86
Fairest of thy sex, and best	28
False though she be to me and love	119
* For me my fair a wreath has wove	186
* Freedom is a real treasure	103
From all uneasy passions free	192
* From place to place forlorn I go	159
* From sweet bewitching tricks of love	104
* G ENTLE Love, this hour befriend me	32
Give me more love, or more disdain	125
Go lovely rose	24
*. Go, rose, my Chloes bosom grace	25
* Go tell Amynta, gentle swain	31
* Grim king of the ghosts make haste	67
* H AIL to the myrtle shade	222
Hard by the hall, our masters house	76
* Hark! hark! 'tis a voice from the tomb	71
Haste, my rein-deer, and let us nimbly go	223
He that loves a rosy cheek	108

INDEX.

Honest lover whatsoever	92
* How bless'd has my time been, what joys have I known	245
* How gentle was my Damons air	54
How hardly I conceal'd my tears	164
I Cannot change, as others do	32
I did but look and love a while	4
I grant, a thousand oaths I swore	139
* I lik'd but never lov'd before	10
* I'll range around the shady bowers	44
I love, I dote, I rave with pain	47
* I love thee, by heavens, I cannot say more	123
I'm not one of your fops, who, to please a coy lass	124
I never saw a face till now	115
* I smile at Love, and all his arts	8
* I told my nymph, I told her true	180
* If all that I love is her face	256
If all the world and love were young	230
If Cupid once the mind possess	163
If in that breast, so good, so pure	29
If Love and Reason ne'er agree	160
If love be life, I long to die	126
* If 'tis joy to wound a lover	119
If wine and music have the pow'r	202
In Chloris all soft charms agree	113
* In love should there meet a fond pair	246
* In the merry month of May	235
* In vain, dear Chloe, you suggest	134
* In vain, Philander, at my feet	263
* In vain you tell your parting lover	15

It

INDEX.

It is not, Celia, in our pow'r	241
* It is not that I love you less	111
KNOW, Celia, (since thou art so proud)	115
LET not Love on me bestow	125
Let the ambitious ever find	188
* Love's a dream of mighty treasure	192
Love's a gentle gen'rous passion	91
Love's no irregular desire	90
MARGARITA first possess'd	140
* Mistaken fair, lay Sherlock by	25
* My banks they are furnish'd with bees	58
* My days have been so wond'rous free	173
* My dear mistress has a heart	209
* My goddess Lydia, heav'nly fair	189
My love was fickle, once, and changing	11
My name is honest Harry	149
* My passion is as mustard strong	151
* My time, o ye Muses, was happily spent	49
* NO more of my Harriot, of Polly, no more	210
Not, Celia, that I juster am	199
Not the soft sighs of vernal gales	199
* O Had I been by fate decreed	181
* O Nancy, wilt thou go with me	219
* O'er moorlands and mountains, rude, barren, and bare	234
* Of all the girls that are so smart	212

* K 3   Of

INDEX.

* Of all the torments, all the cares	58
Of Leinster, fam'd for maidens fair	78
* Oft on the troubled oceans face	101
Oh! forbear to bid me slight her	6
Oh! how vain is every blessing	92
* Old Chaucer once to this re-echoing grove	105
On Belvideras bosom lying	190
* On the brow of a hill a young shepherdess dwelt	168
* Once more I'll tune the vocal shell	193
Once more Loves mighty charms are broke	117
* One night when all the village slept	69
* Over the mountains	99
P HILLIS, men say that all my vows	179
* S AW you the nymph whom I adore?	21
Say, lovely dream, where could'st thou find	42
* Say, mighty Love, and teach my song	250
* Say, Myra, why is gentle love	14
* Send back my long-stray'd eyes to me	257
Shall I, like an hermit, dwell	129
Shall I, wasting in despair	127
* She, whom above myself I prize	255
Should some perverse malignant star	135
* Sigh no more ladies, sigh no more	262
Sighing and languishing I lay	178
* Stella and Flavia, ev'ry hour	206
* Stella, darling of the Muses	174
* Sweet are the banks when spring perfumes	185
* Sweet are the charms of her I love	171

* TAKE,

INDEX.

* TAKE, oh! take, those lips away	23
Tell me, Damon, dost thou languish	94
Tell me no more how fair she is	22
Tell me not I my time misspend	184
* That Jenny's my friend, my delight, and my pride	243
That which her slender waist confin'd	171
* The bird that hears her nestlings cry	191
The charms which blooming beauty shows	264
The flame of love asswages	101
* The gentle swan, with graceful pride	200
* The heavy hours are almost past	37
* The merchant to secure his treasure	133
* The nymph that undoes me is fair and unkind	22
The shape alone let others prize	207
* The silver moons enamour'd beam	195
* The silver rain, the pearly dew	29
* The sun was sunk beneath the hill	46
* The western sky was purpled o'er	196
* Think not, my love, when secret grief	257
* Thou rising sun, whose gladsome ray	216
* Though cruel you seem to my pain	39
Though, Flavia, to my warm desire	110
* Though winter its desolate train	238
* Thus Kitty, beautiful and young	204
'Tis not your saying that you love	30
'Tis now, since I sat down before	131
* To all you ladies now at land	34
* To be gazing on those charms	191
* To melancholy thoughts a prey	33, 259
* To the brook and the willow that heard him complain	52
* Tom loves Mary passing well	144

* K 4   * Too

INDEX.

* Too plain, dear youth, these tell-tale eyes	166
* 'Twas when the seas were roaring	73
VAIN are the charms of white and red	109
* Vain is ev'ry fond endeavour	262
* WAFT me, some soft and cooling breeze	218
* We all to conquering beauty bow	183
* Well met, pretty nymph, says a jolly young swain	145
What fury does disturb my rest	40
What state of life can be so blest	41
When charming Teraminta sings	203
* When Damon languish'd at my feet	168
* When Delia on the plain appears	175
When fair Serrena first I knew	27
* When first I fair Celinda knew	26
* When first I saw thee graceful move	3
When first upon your tender cheek	2
When gentle Celia first I knew	137
* When here, Lucinda, first we came	225
* When innocence and beauty meet	208
When lovely woman stoops to folly	170
When Phillis watch'd her harmless sheep	158
* When the trees are all bare, not a leaf to be seen	232
When youth, my Celia, 's in the prime	239
Where the light cannot pierce, in a grove of tall trees	231
* While from my looks, fair nymph, you guess	6
Whilst I am scorch'd with hot desire	30
Whilst on those lovely looks I gaze	9
White as her hand, fair Julia threw	7

* Why,

INDEX.

* Why, cruel creature, why so bent	45
* Why, Delia, ever when I gaze	16
* Why d'ye with such disdain refuse	116
Why so pale and wan, fond lover	130
Why we love, and why we hate	143
Why will Florella, when I gaze	14
* Why will you my passion reprove	60
With women I have pass'd my days	12
Wrong not, sweet mistress of my heart	18
* YE belles, and ye flirts, and ye pert little things	252
* Ye fair married dames, who so often deplore	248
* Ye fair possess'd of every charm	249
* Ye happy swains, whose hearts are free	103
* Ye little Loves, that round her wait	131
* Ye shepherds, give ear to my lay	62
* Ye shepherds so chearful and gay	56
* Ye virgin pow'rs, defend my heart	261
Yes, Daphne, in your face I find	112
Yes, fairest proof of beautys pow'r	39
* Yes I'm in love, I feel it now	211
You may cease to complain	19
* You say, at your feet I have wept in despair	114

INDEX.

VOLUME II.

PART II.

(DRINKING-SONGS.)

	Page
A BOOK, a friend, a song, a glafs	6
Adieu, ye jovial youths, who join	77
* As fwift as time put round the glafs	17
* BACCHUS muft now his power refign	43
Better our heads than hearts fhould ake	2
* Bid me, when forty winters more	9
* Bufy, curious, thirfty Fly	17
* By the gayly circling glafs	39
*COME, come, my hearts of gold	54
Come fill me a glafs, fill it high	33
* Come now, all ye focial powers	11
* Cupid no more fhall give me grief	339
*DEAR Tom, this brown jug, that now foams with	73
* Diogenes furly and proud	34

* EVERY

INDEX.

* **E**VERY man take his glafs in his hand   21

* **F**ILL me a bowl, a mighty bowl   40

* **G**AY Bacchus, liking Eftcourts wine   47
    * Give me but a friend and a glafs, boys   9
* God profper long from being broke   50

* **H**AD Neptune, when firft he took charge of the fea   23
    * Hence with cares, complaints and frowning   342
* How ftands the glafs around   340

* **I** Am the king and prince of drinkers   44
    * I cannot eate but lytle meate   71
* If gold could lengthen life, I fwear   13
I have been in love, and in debt and in drink   74

* **J**OLLY mortals, fill your glaffes   16

* **L**ET foldiers fight for pay and praife   42
    * Let us drink and be merry   14
* Let's be jovial, fill our glaffes   20
Liften all, I pray   28

MORTALS, learn your lives to meafure   19
    * My temples with clufters of grapes I'll entwine   75

NOT drunken, nor fober, but neighbour to both   58
    * Now Phœbus finketh in the weft   38

* **O**LD Chiron thus preach'd to his pupil Achilles   19

                                               * PHO!

INDEX.

PHO! pox o' this nonsense, I prithee give o'er	1
* Preach not to me your musty rules	11
* **R**AIL no more, ye learned asses	34
* **S**AYS Plato, why should man be vain	8
* She tells me with claret she cannot agree	5
* Some say women are like the seas	3
* **T**HE festive board was met, the social band	341
* The man that is drunk is void of all care	46
The thirsty earth drinks up the rain	24
* The women all tell me I'm false to my lass	3
* This bottle's the sun of our table	39
* **U**PBRAID me not, capricious fair	74
* **V**ULCAN, contrive me such a cup	39
* **W**HAT Cato advises most certainly wise is	12
When Bacchus, jolly god, invites	342
* When I drain the rosy bowl	18
* When the chill sirocco blows	37
Whilst some in epic strains delight	68
Wine, wine in a morning	22
* With an honest old friend, and a merry old song	6
* With women and wine I defy every care	76
* **Y**E good fellows all	25
* Ye true honest Britons who love your own land	56
You know that our ancient philosophers hold	41
* Youth's the season made for joys	10
* **Z**ENO, Plato, Aristotle	38

INDEX.

VOLUME II.

PART III.

(MISCELLANEOUS SONGS.)

	Page
* **A**S near Porto-Bello lying	176
* **B**LOW, blow, thou winter wind	117
* **C**EASE rude Boreas, bluſt'ring railer!	127
* Come, come, my good ſhepherds,	94
* Come follow, follow me	157
Come ſhepherds, we'll follow the hearſe	149
* **F**ORTH from my dark and diſmal cell	146
Friendſhip, peculiar gift of Heaven	115
* From Oberon in Fairy-land	160
* From the court to the cottage convey me away	100
* **G**ENTLY ſtir and blow the fire	136
Go ſoul, the bodys gueſt	117
* Goddeſs of eaſe, leave Lethes brink	99
HAPPY inſect, what can be	164
* Hark! hark! jolly ſportsmen, a while to my tale	168
* How happy a ſtate does the miller poſſeſs	108

How

INDEX.

How happy is he born and taught	87
* How pleasant a sailors life passes	106
How sacred and how innocent	95
How sleep the brave, who sink to rest	151
I Envy not the mighty great	88
I envy not the proud their wealth	86
* If I live to grow old, as I find I go down	109
* In good king Charleses golden days	125
In Tyburn-road a man there liv'd	173
LO! here, beneath this hallow'd shade	159
MAN's a poor deluded bubble	104
* My mind to me a kingdom is	81
NO glory I covet, no riches I want	89
* Nor on beds of fading flowers	92
O Memory! thou fond deceiver	135
* O say, what is that thing call'd light	104
Oft I've implor'd the gods in vain	154
PRINCES that rule and empire sway	101
SLEEP, sleep poor youth, sleep, sleep in peace	150
Some hoist up Fortune to the skies	90
* Songs of shepherds, in rustical roundelays	165
* THE glories of our birth and state	91
* The honest heart whose thoughts are clear	109

* The

INDEX.

* The muse and the hero together are fir'd	179
* The solitary bird of night	111
The sweet and blushing rose	103
* The world, my dear Myra, is full of deceit	116
* The wretch condemn'd with life to part	135
* Thou soft flowing Avon, by thy silver stream	153
Through groves sequester'd, dark, and still	99
* Thursday in the morn, the ides of May	181
* To fair Fideles grassy tomb	152
* To hug yourself in perfect ease	85
To tinkling brooks, to twilight shades	93
* Two gossips they merrily met	137
* UNDER the greenwood tree	145
* WELCOME, welcome brother debtor	105
What frenzy must his soul possess	93
What is th' existence of mans life?	102
* What man in his wits had not rather be poor	88
* When daffodils begin to peer	143
* When daysies pied, and violets blue	144
* When isicles hang on the wall	144
* When Orpheus went down to the regions below	137
When this old cap was new	121
* Who has e'er been at Paris must needs know the *Greve*	171
* With an old song made by an old ancient pate	140
Would we attain the happiest state	84
* YOU gentlemen of England	130

INDEX.
VOLUME II.
PART IV.
(ANCIENT BALLADS.)

	Page
ALL youths of fair England	255
As it fell one holyday	215
As it fell out upon a day	188
*COLD and raw the North did blow	286
*GOD prosper long our noble king	326
HENRY, our royal king, would ride a hunting	272
*IF Rosamond, that was so fair	228
* I'll tell you a story, a story anon	282
In the days of old	237
Is there never a man in all Scotland	322
LORD Thomas he was a bold forester	185

MARK

INDEX.

M ARK well my heavy doleful tale   209

*N OW ponder well, you parents dear   249

*O F a worthy London prentice   301
   * Old stories tell how Hercules   307

T HERE was a youth, and a well belov'd youth   234

W AS ever knight for ladys sake   296
    When Arthur first in court began   291
When as king Henry rul'd this land   220
When Flora with her fragrant flowers   313
* When Troy town, for ten years wars,   199
Will you hear a Spanish lady   205

Y OU beauteous ladies, great and small   244
    You dainty dames, so finely fram'd   194

NAMES
OF
AUTHORS,

IN BOTH VOLUMES;

WITH REFERENCES.

ADDISON, MR.	VOL. I. Page 11. 119.
AIKIN, MISS	I. 95. 137.
AKENSIDE, DR.	I. 207.
BAKER, MR.	I. 181.
BARBAULD, MRS. See AIKIN, MISS.	
BATH, EARL OF. See PULTENEY.	
BEAUMONT, FRANCIS	II. 28, 58.
BEDINGFIELD, MR. W.	II. 85.
BEHN, MRS.	I. 30. 167.
BERKELEY, ———, ESQ.	I. 237.
BICKERSTAFF, MR. ISAAC	I. 246. II. 109.
BOOTH, MR. BARTON	I. 171.
BREREWOOD, THOMAS, ESQ.	I. 231, 232.
BRETON, NICHOLAS	I. 235.
BROME, ALEXANDER	II. 74.
BROOKE, LORD. See GREVILL.	
BROWN, TOM	II. 22.
BUCKINGHAM, DUKE OF	I. 118, 177, 178, 192.
BUDGELL, EUSTACE, ESQ.	I. 124.
BULTEEL, JOHN	I. 121, 139.
BURNABY, CHARLES	I. 203.
BYROM, DR.	I. 49.

CAREW,

NAMES OF AUTHORS.

CAREW, THOMAS, ESQ.	I. 108, 115, 125.
CAREY, HARRY	I. 21, 39, 44, 91, 101, 191, 212, 255.
	II. 6, 12, 38, 43, 100, 339.
CARTER, MISS	II. 111.
CHESTERFIELD, EARL OF	I. 25.
CHICHESTER, BISHOP OF. See KING.	
CHURCHILL, MR. CHARLES	I. 239.
CIBBER, COLLEY, ESQ.	II. 104.
COCKBURN, MRS.	I. 5.
COFFEY, MR.	II. 105.
COLLINS, MR.	II. 151, 152.
CONCANEN, MR. MATTHEW	I. 123.
CONGREVE, MR.	I. 119.
COWLEY, ABRAHAM, ESQ.	I. 140. II. 24, 164.
CROXALL, DR.	I. 218.
CUNNINGHAM, MR. JOHN	I. 195, 200, 234. II. 149.
DALTON, DR.	I. 54. II. 11, 39, 92.
DAVISON, FRANCIS	I. 126. II. 117.
DAWSON, ARTHUR, ESQ.	II. 25.
DODSLEY, MR. ROBERT	II. 104.
DORSET, EARL OF	I. 34, 188.
DRYDEN, MR.	I. 31, 41, 86, 89, 122.
D'URFEY, TOM	II. 5, 150.
EATON, SIR JOHN	I. 184.
ETHEREGE, SIR GEORGE	I. 103, 158, 241.
FAWKES, REV. MR.	II. 73.
FITZGERALD, REV. MR. THOMAS	I. 264. II. 89.

*L 2 GARRICK

NAMES of AUTHORS.

GARRICK, MR.	I. 186, 193, 246. II. 56, 94, 153.
GAY, MR.	I. 25, 73, 151, 214. II. 10.
GLOVER, MR.	II. 181.
GOLDSMITH, DR.	I. 170. II. 135.
GREVILL, SIR FULKE, LORD BROOKE	I. 120.
GREVILLE, MRS.	I. 155.
HAWKESWORTH, DR.	II. 99.
HIGHMORE, MR. CHARLES	II. 108.
HILL, AARON, ESQ.	I. 6, 32.
HOOLE, MR.	II. 93.
HOW, MR. JOHN	I. 113.
JACOB, HILDEBRAND, ESQ.	II. 88.
JENYNS, SOAME, ESQ.	I. 77, 166.
JOHNSON, DR.	I. 199, 240.
JONES, MISS MARY	I. 168.
JONSON, BEN	II. 42.
KING, DR. HENRY, BP. OF CHICHESTER	I. 22. II. 102.
LANSDOWN, LORD	I. 45.
LEE, NAT	I. 222.
LILLO, MR. GEORGE	II. 103.
LISLE, DR.	II. 137.
LLOYD, MR. ROBERT	I. 238.
LYTTELTON, LORD	I. 14, 37, 175.
MARLOW, CHRISTOPHER	I. 228.
MENDEZ, MR. MOSES	I. 114, 262.

MIDDLESEX,

NAMES of AUTHORS.

MIDDLESEX, EARL OF	I. 225.
MILTON	II. 238.
MOLESWORTH, VISCOUNT	I. 4.
MONTAGUE, LADY MARY WORTLEY	I. 159.
MOORE, MR. EDWARD	I. 71, 168, 226, 243, 245.
MOORE, SIR JOHN	I. 29, 186.
OLDHAM, MR.	II. 40.
OTWAY, MR.	I. 4, 47, 66. II. 101.
PARNELL, DR.	I. 173. II. 47.
PARRAT, MR.	I. 87.
PERCY, DR.	I. 219.
PHILIPS, AMBROSE, ESQ.	I. 143, 188.
PHILIPS, MRS. KATHERINE	II. 95.
PILKINGTON, MRS.	I. 33, 174. II. 86.
POPE, DR. WALTER	II. 109.
PRIOR, MATHEW, ESQ.	I. 15, 30, 39, 75, 133, 136, 202, 204. II. 171.
PULTENEY, WILLIAM, ESQ. (EARL OF BATH)	I. 109.
RALEIGH, SIR WALTER	I. 18, 129, 230.
ROCHESTER, EARL OF	I. 9, 32, 189, 209, 236. II. 39.
ROWE, NICHOLAS, ESQ.	I. 52, 64.
SCROOPE, SIR CAR	I. 69.
SEDLEY, SIR CHARLES	I. 117, 157, 179, 199.
SEWARD, REV. MR.	I. 27.
SHAKSPEARE	I. 262. II. 117, 143, 144, 145.

NAMES OF AUTHORS.

SHENSTONE, WILLIAM, ESQ.   I. 56, 81, 180, 196. II. 77.
SHERIDAN, RICHARD BRINSLEY, ESQ.   I. 258. II. 39.
SHIRLEY, JAMES   -   II. 91.
SMART, MR. CHRISTOPHER   I. 105, 210. II. 99.
SOUTHERN, MR.   I. 11.
STEEL, SIR RICHARD   I. 125, 159, 216, 223.
STEVENS, MR. GEORGE ALEXANDER   II. 127.
SUCKLING, SIR JOHN   I. 92, 130, 131.

THEOBALD, MR.   I. 101.
THOMPSON, MR. WILLIAM   II. 6.
TICKELL, THOMAS, ESQ.   I. 78.

VANBROOK, MR.   I. 116.
VANBRUGH, SIR JOHN   I. 8.

WALLER, EDMUND, ESQ.   I. 24, 43, 111, 171.
WALSH, WILLIAM, ESQ.   I. 38, 40, 148.
WARTON, REV. MR. THOMAS   II. 93.
WATTS, ISAAC, D. D.   I. 250.
WESLEY, REV. MR. SAMUEL   II. 88.
WHARTON, DUKE OF   II. 50.
WHARTON, MRS.   I. 164.
WHATELEY, MISS   I. 220.
WHITEHEAD, WILLIAM, ESQ.   I. 211, 252.
WHITEHEAD, PAUL, ESQ.   II. 342.
WILLIAMS, MRS. A.   II. 115.
WILLIAMS, SIR CHARLES HANBURY   I. 202.
WINCHELSEA, COUNTESS OF   II. 84.
WITHER, GEORGE   I. 127.

WODHULL,

NAMES OF AUTHORS.

WODHULL, MICHAEL, ESQ.   I. 28.
WOLSELEY, ROBERT, ESQ.   I. 17, 103.
WOTTON, SIR HENRY   II. 87.
WOTY, MR. WILLIAM   I. 185. II. 75, 76.

YONGE, SIR WILLIAM   I. 134.

CORRECTIONS AND ADDITIONAL NOTES.

VOLUME I.

PAGE 6. *add* BY MATHEW PRIOR ESQ.

P. 11. Song XIV. *add* BY MR. SOUTHERN, *with this note,* In The Difappointment, or Mother in fafhion.

P. 27. Song XXXII. *add* BY THE REV. MR. SEWARD.

P. 29. Song XXXV. *This fong has been afcribed to dr. Johnfon, but, it is believed, without foundation.*

P. 32. Song XL. l. 15. *for* foul *r.* pulfe.

P. 40. Song XLVIII. *add* BY WILLIAM WALSH ESQ.

P. 46. Song LIII. *Has appeared under the name of mr. Gay; and quære if his?*

P. 49. Song LV. The lady the fubject of this ballad, was the eldeſt daughter of the famous Dr. Richard Bentley, and a univerfity beauty at the time when the author was at college; ſhe was married to Dr. Richard Cumberland, late biſhop of Kilmore, and died a few years ago. HAWKINS (*Hiſt. Muſ.* V. 98. *Where ſee other muſic to it by dr. Croft*).

P. 67. Song LXI. THE LUNATIC LOVER.

P. 76. Song LXVII. *This ballad does not appear to have been known before its communication to lord Oxford by mr. Prior, who tells his lordſhip he found it in a cottage in Lancaſhire. It may, therefor, not improbably, be the compoſition of that excellent poet, of whoſe pen it is by no means unworthy.*

P. 97. l. 4. *for* love *r.* live. *This line is certainly faulty, though all the copies agree in giving it as here printed. Inſtead of* thou doſt, *the Author probably wrote* doſt not.

P. 101. Sung XIII. *add* BY MR. THEOBALD.

P. 105. Song XIX. *The air of this cantata is likewiſe an imitation of a poem aſcribed to Chaucer.*

P. 114. Song VIII. l. ult. *for* patience *r.* conſcience.

P. 121. l. 3. foſter.] *A very old contraction of* forefter, *much uſed by Spenſer, and other ancient writers.*

P. 121.

CORRECTIONS AND ADDITIONAL NOTES.

P. 121. Song XVI. *John Bulteel appears to have been secretary to the earl of Clarendon, and to have died in 1669. See Bio. Drama. i. 51.*

P. 132. l. 20. *for* been *r.* bin. *Many of the old poets, in imitation of Spenser, adopted a strange and licentious method of altering both the orthography and pronunciation of words to suit their versification. Some of these faults are incorrigible, and this seems to be one. See also* ariant *in Davisons Song, ii. 17. and* than *and* emperess *in Cowleys Chronicle, i. 140.*

P. 144. Song XXXVI. *Is an imitation of the Sixth Idyllium of Moschus. See Fawkeses Translation, p. 284.*

P. 146. Humphrey Gubbin *is a clownish character in Steels* Tender Husband, *in which this song may have been originally sung. One of the thoughts, however, is from the Old Batchelor of Congreve.*

P. 151. l. 4. *add an* O.

P. 157. Song I. *Mr. Nichols, in his collection of poems, gives this* " From the French of Madame de la Suze," *by Sir Car Scroope.*

P. 183. *(correct the first figure)* Song XI. *add* THE PERFECTION, *with this note,* Originally addressed To the [first] Duchess of Grafton.

P. 184. l. 1. (*of the song*) *for* misspend *r.* misspend.

P. 186. note. *Instead of* At the end of - *r.* In - Mr. Twisses tour in Spain. *The song itself is at the end.*

P. 191. Honest Harry *introduced this song with a slight alteration, as a duet, in his little Interlude of* Nancy or the Parting Lovers. *It appears however (from his poems) to have been written long before.*

P. 193. Song XXIV. *The real object of the poets admiration was said to be* mrs. Woffington, *the actress.*

P. 203. Song XXXII. *The Author, according to Bysshe, was* [CHARLES] BURNABY.

P. 206. Song XXXIV. *This is printed as* mrs. Barbers *in her poems (London, 1734. 4to.), and appears in Dodsleys collection under the name of* J. Earle. *As to* mrs. Barber, *she could not write so well, and* mr. Earle *seems to be a fictitious personage. It was restored to* mrs. Pilkington, *on the authority of* mr. Deane Swift. *See Nicholses Supplement to Swift,* iii. 247. *It is almost needless to say that the song has been designed to pay a compliment to* mrs. Johnson.

P. 214. l. 1. *for* pounds *r.* pound.

P. 216. Song XLII. *Sir Richard is said to have written all the Spectators under the signature* T; *and, if so, should be author of this song*

CORRECTIONS AND ADDITIONAL NOTES.

song and the other at p. 223. But the elegance of the former, at least, seems, it must be confessed, more characteristic of the peculiarly happy manner of mr. Addison.

P. 228. note. Marlow had for rival an ill-looking fellow, whom, in a paroxysm of jealousy and revenge, he attempted to stab; but the fellow, seizing his hand, forced him to strike his dagger into his own head.

P. 237. Song VIII. It has been said that this song was written for the once well known lady Vane.

P. 253. Song LXXII. This agreable little piece is inserted in a Collection of Miscellanies published under the name of Anna Williams, a blind lady; containing some poems written by herself, and many more by dr. Johnson, and by mrs. Thrale, Percy, Goldsmith, and others, whom the doctor, from motives of charity, invited to contribute to it. The generosity of one of these gentlemen is rather remarkable: he very modestly suffered mrs. Williams to take the credit of several things which he had published a dozen times before under his own name.

P. 257. Think not, my love, &c.] The tender sweetness of these beautiful stanzas, which are among the Six Ballads composed and published by mr. Linley, will sufficiently indicate the elegant pen of the author of The School for Scandal.

Ibid. Send back, &c.] A very judicious alteration, and real improvement, of The Message by dr. Donne.

VOLUME II.

P. 5. Song V. *Honest Tom's* title to this song is rather questionable. In one of his plays he has a song beginning,

When I visit proud Celia just come from the glass,

which is so near the present as to make one thing certain while it leaves it doubtful, i. e. either that the present copy was borrowed from Tom, or that Tom borrowed from it.

P. 9. Song X. Quære if not BY SIR JOHN HILL?

P. 12. Song XIV. add BY HARRY CAREY, which familiar appellative the reader is desired to prefer in every place to the more stately one of MR. HENRY.

CORRECTIONS AND ADDITIONAL NOTES.

HENRY. *Cato's real advice (whoever he was) is comprised in the following distich, prefixed by honest Harry, in his* Musical Century, *as a motto to the song;*

   Interpone tuis interdum gaudia curis,
   Ut possis animo quemvis sufferre laborem. *Distich. lib. 3.*

Which sage and social precept is thus excellently translated by master John Hoole, of indefatigable memory:

   Mirth with thy labour sometimes put in ure,
   That better thou thy labour may'st endure.

P. 15. l. 7. *for* bnt *r.* but.

P. 19. l. 4. *add this note.* Mr. Fawkeses translation contains the following additional lines, necessarily omitted when it was converted into a song:

   When the foaming bowl I drain,
   Real blessings are my gain;
   Blessings which my own I call:
   Death is common to us all.

Ibid. Song XXI. l. 10. *for* Loosing *r.* Losing.

P. 22. Song XXV. THE WHET. *It is printed in Tom's works; but that, indeed, is no conclusive proof of his property in it.*

P. 28. Song XXIX. *This song is inserted in Beaumont's poems, and his name is here prefixed to it on the authority of an old manuscript copy in the Harleian library.*

P. 28. l. 6. *for* desertum *r.* disertum.

P. 31. l. 6. *for* tantnm *r.* tantum.

P. 33. Song XXX. BY MR. PHILIPS. Mr. Nichols, *from many circumstances, has little doubt but this convival song was by the author of* The Splendid Shilling. *See his* Select Collection of Poems, iv. 281. *But it seems to have appeared at a too early period to be safely ascribed to that writer. It is more probably the production of that Philips who was nephew to Milton, and author of the* Theatrum Poetarum *and several poetical performances.*

Ibid. l. 8. *for* merry *r.* merrily.

P. 39. *for* XXVI. *r.* XXXVI.

Ibid. Song XXXVII. *add* FROM ANACREON.

P. 40. Song XXXVIII. *add* BY MR. OLDHAM. *It is part of a long poem.*

P. 42.

CORRECTIONS and ADDITIONAL NOTES.

P. 42. Song XL. *This is not found in Jonson's works, and D'Urfey, who furnished the name, might possibly mean Ben Johnson the player, his own cotemporary. But, whoever was the author, the song was certainly written before the Restoration.*

P. 46. *for* XLII. *r.* XLIII. *This song should have been mentioned as a parody of the twenty-second ode of the second book of Horace.*

P. 57. Song XLVIII. l. 1. Sirocco.] *So the modern copies. All the old ones read* Charokkoe. *The Sirocco (Ital. Scirocco) is the south east wind, and would perhaps be more properly written and pronounced* Shirocco.

P. 58. l. 9. *for* laaghter *r.* laughter.

Ibid. Song XLIX. *Is to be found in Beaumont's poems, and may, on that authority, be assigned to him as its author. It appears, however, from the following extract, to have been once filiated upon a much bigger personage.*

The veriest straws (like that of father Garnet) are shewn to the world as admirable reliques, if the least strokes of the image of a celebrated author does but seem to be upon them. The press hath been injurious in this kind to the memory of Bishop Andrews, to whom it owed a deep and solemn reverence. It hath sent forth a pamphlet upon an idle subject, under the venerable name of that great man; who (like the grass in hot countries, of which they are wont to say that it groweth hay) was born grave and sober: and, still farther to aggravate the injury, it hath given to that idle subject the idler title of THE EX-ALE-TATION OF ALE. *Lord Bacons works,* 1730. *Vol.* I. (*Account of the Edition, p.* 180.)

P. 63. l. 5. *for* beer *r.* peer.

P. 67. l. 9. *for* whether *r.* whither.

P. 68. *for* LI. *r.* L. *and correct the following numbers accordingly.*

Ibid. *Some editions*] i. e. *The spurious ones published by mr.* Bell, *bookseller in the Strand.*

Ibid. l. 2. invite] *So the copies;* quæ. indite?

P. 76. l. 3. (of the song) *r.* Each.

P. 84. *after* l. 6. *r.* V. O.

P. 88. Song VII. *add* BY THE REV. MR. SAMUEL WESLEY.

P. 89. Song VIII. *add* BY THE REV. MR. THOMAS FITZGERALD.

CORRECTIONS AND ADDITIONAL NOTES.

P. 94. Song XIV. l. 3 and 4, guiltless] *So the best copies. It is usually sung guileless, even at Drury-lane theatre. The alteration was probably made by the Composer.*

P. 95. Song XV. *for* CELEBRATED *r.* MATCHLESS.

P. 100. Song XVIII. BY HARRY CAREY, *who intitles it* Mrs. Stuarts Retirement.

P. 101. Song XIX. *add* BY MR. OTWAY, *with this note,* In the tragedy of Alcibiades.

P. 105. Song XXIV. BY MR. COFFEY.

P. 108. Song XXVI. *This song was written - not by* MR. DODSLEY, *but - by a* MR. CHARLES HIGHMORE, *at his request.*

P. 115. Song XXX. BY MRS. A. WILLIAMS?

P. 117. Song XXXIII. *This song is here printed from the second edition of Davisons poems (1611, 12mo.). Dr. Percy appears to have made use of a later, and, as it should seem, more accurate edition, in 1624, and by his copy (which, could his fidelity be relied on, would have been entirely followed) some palpable mistakes have been rectified. The passages corrected are left distinguished by ' commas.'*

P. 130. Song XXXVII. *This is altered from an older ballad, written by Martin Parker, an early printed copy of which, in black letter, under the title of* Saylors for my money . . . . . To the tune of the Iouiall Cobler, *is in the Pepysian library.*

P. 150. note. *for* Eales *r.* Eccles.

P. 157. Song LV. l. 3. *for* oe'r *r.* o'er.

P. 160. Song LVII. Dr. Percy has, among his old ballads, given this excellent song, with his usual correctness, from an ancient black letter copy in the British Museum." *After it was printed off, as he acquaints us in a note, he saw* an ancient black letter copy containing some variations, and intitled, " The merry pranks of Robin-Good-fellow. To the tune of Dulcina, &c." To this copy, *says he,* were prefixed two wooden cuts of ROBIN GOOD-FELLOW, which seem to represent the dresses in which this whimsical character was formerly exhibited on the stage. To gratify the curious *he has caused these figures to be very neatly engraved. And his numerous readers seem to have given implicit credit to every thing he has been pleased to tell them. For* THEIR *better information, however, it may not be impertinent to let them into a few secrets.*

1. *The*

CORRECTIONS AND ADDITIONAL NOTES.

1. *The ancient black letter copy of this ballad in the Muſeum, whence the learned and ingenious editor expreſsly declares he printed it, has the identical figures and title which he pretends to have afterwards diſcovered.*

2. *Neither of the ſaid figures has the ſlighteſt connection either with the whimſical character perſonated in the ſong, or with ſtage repreſentation: both of them having been originally deſigned for, and the identical blocks made uſe of in* Bulwers Artificial Changeling (*p.* 460 & 472)*: the firſt being intended for one of the black and white gallants of* Sealebay, *adorned with the moon, ſtars,* &c. *the other for a hairy ſavage.*

P. 163. l. 13. fet] i. e. *fetch.*

Whom ſtraunge adventure did from Britaine FETT.
          Faerie Queene, III. i. 8.

The leacher that had ſtaide—
Impacient of his flame
And beaſtly heat, to FET the wench
Himſelfe in perſon came.
          Turberviles Tragical Tales. 1587. *Hiſt.* 2.

And I wyll go FET hyther a cōpany
That ye ſhall here thē ſyng as ſwetly
As they were 'angelles' clere.
          O. Play of The iiii. elements. *Sig.* E. iii.

That did the freers from us FET.
          Ballad of Luther, &c. Reliques, ii. 117.

It is more generally uſed for fetched.

P. 163. l. 22. heyday guiſe] i. e. *Heydeguies, country dances. As in Draytons* Poly-Olbion, Song 25.

Dance many a merry round, and many a HYDEGY.

P. 189. note. *See a very elegant and particular account of this famous ſea fight, in ſir John Dalrymples Memoirs, Vol.* I. *p.* 503. *and mr. Macpherſons Hiſtory, Vol.* II. *p.* 11.

P. 215. Ballad VII. *Is here printed from a copy preſerved in Drydens Collection of Miſcellaneous Poems: The identical authority, without doubt, which the learned and ingenious editor, or rather author, of the* Reliques of Ancient Engliſh Poetry *has there followed; though, from the affected parade of the antiquary, ever ſtudious to conceal the real, if modern, ſources of information, it is pretended to be given (with the aſſiſtance of his folio MS.) from an old printed copy in the Britiſh Muſeum.*

CORRECTIONS AND ADDITIONAL NOTES.

In the Pepys collection, *says he*, is an imitation of this old song, in a different measure, by a more modern pen, with many alterations, but evidently for the worse. *Would any person suspect that the copies in the Museum (for there are two) were no more than much later impressions of this very imitation? But it is even so. The criticism is notwithstanding just. And had the reverend gentleman actually consulted his authority, it is scarcely probable he would have referred to it. The several old pieces preserved in the above Miscellany appear to have been printed with fidelity, at least; and it may be remembered that few black letter copies now extant are more ancient than mr. Drydens own memory.*

P. 233. l. 22. Shoreditch.] *In this particular, at least, either mrs. Shore, or the writer who furnished her with the information, is under a small mistake, Shoreditch having existed, by that very name, for some hundreds of years before she was born; being part of, or near to, the great common shore (sewer) or drain of the city.*

P. 234. Ballad X. Islington] Islington in Norfolk is probably the place here meant. PERCY.

P. 237. Ballad XI. The story of this ballad seems to be taken from an incident in the domestic history of Charles the Bald, king of France. His daughter Judith was betrothed to Ethelwulph, king of England; but before the marriage was consummated, Ethelwulph died, and she returned to France; whence she was carried off by Baldwyn, Forester of Flanders; who after many crosses and difficulties, at length obtained the kings consent to their marriage, and was made Earl of Flanders. This happened about A. D. 863.---See Rapin, Henault, and the French Historians. PERCY.

P. 282. Ballad XVI. *The reader must necessarily excuse the miserably corrupt state in which the editor is obliged to present this ballad. It has doubtless originally possessed some merit, which, if an older copy than those already consulted should happen to cast up, may hereafter be restored. In the mean time, it may be perused in the utmost perfection in the* Reliques of ancient English Poetry. *The original composition so judiciously interwoven into this and almost every other old poem in the above elegant collection evinces so much ingenuity, niceness, genius, and critical taste, that the reverend author certainly merits the bays as a poet, as much as he deserves the lash as an editor.*

P. 313.

CORRECTIONS AND ADDITIONAL NOTES.

P. 313. Ballad XXII. *The story of this ballad is to be found in most of the English chronicles under the year 1511.*

P. 322. Ballad XXIII. *The best account of Armstrong, his conduct, capture, and execution,---for, alas! instead of ending his life so gallantly as he is made to do in the song, he was ignobly hanged upon a gallows,--is given by Lindsay of Pitscottie, in his History of Scotland. (Edin. 1727. folio). He is likewise noticed by Buchanan.*

P. 326. Ballad XXIV. *This ballad appears to have been modernized about the time of James or Charles I. from an ancient piece upon the same subject, preserved by Hearne, (Guliel. Neubri. I. lxxxii.) and, thence, (not very faithfully or correctly) printed by Percy, beginning,*

The Perse owt off Northombarlande and a vowe to God mayd he.

An admirable Latin version, written at the command of dr. Compton, bishop of London, by mr. Henry Bold, is inserted among that gentlemans Latin Songs, and in Drydens Collection of Miscellaneous Poems.

P. 334. l. 15.   And when they rung the evening bell
                   The battle scarce was done.

That is, *says Percy*, the Curfew bell, usually rung at eight o'clock. *But this ingenious conjecture happens, unfortunately, to be an egregious mistake. The evening bell is the bell for vespers, or six o'clock prayers, as the learned commentator might have observed in transcribing or printing the original ballad, which expresly tells us, that*

when EVEN SONG BELL was rang the battell was nat half done.

That it was formerly looked upon as an uncommon, and, perhaps, irreligious circumstance, for a Christian army to continue engaged after the ringing of this bell, appears from a similar passage in the ancient Spanish romance of TIRANT LO BLANCH *(Barcelona, 1497. folio); where it is said,* " E continuant toste'ps la batailla era ia quasi hora de vespres, &c." (Capitol clvii.) " L'heure de Vêpres approchoit, & le combat duroit " encore." (Traduc. Fran. i. 293.)

DIRECTIONS to the BINDER.

VOL. I.

The Historical Essay, notwithstanding it is marked Vol. II. is to follow the Preface.

Page 264 concludes the Volume.

VOL. II.

Page 342 concludes the Volume.

VOL. III.

Consists of the Music, in Two Parts, at the End of which are to be placed the Indexes Sheets *K *L.

When the Work is directed to be bound in Two Volumes, the Music must be placed at the End of the Volume to which it respectively belongs; and Sheets *K *L after the Music in the Second Volume.

The Binder is desired to be particularly careful in folding and placing the Leaves that contain Plates, and to put Paper before each Plate.

www.ingramcontent.com/pod-product-compliance
Lightning Source LLC
Chambersburg PA
CBHW021154230426
43667CB00006B/386